11-16-04

MODERN WORLD NATIONS

MODERN WORLD NATIONS

Costa Rica

Roger Dendinger
South Dakota School of Mines and Technology

Series Consulting Editor
Charles F. Gritzner
South Dakota State University

CHELSEA HOUSE
PUBLISHERS
A Haights Cross Communications Company

Philadelphia

Frontispiece: Flag of Costa Rica

Cover: Costa Rican beach

CHELSEA HOUSE PUBLISHERS

VP, NEW PRODUCT DEVELOPMENT Sally Cheney
DIRECTOR OF PRODUCTION Kim Shinners
CREATIVE MANAGER Takeshi Takahashi
MANUFACTURING MANAGER Diann Grasse

Staff for COSTA RICA

EDITOR Lee Marcott
PRODUCTION EDITOR Jaimie Winkler
PICTURE RESEARCH 21st Century Publishing and Communications, Inc.
COVER DESIGNER Keith Trego, SERIES DESIGNER Takeshi Takahashi
LAYOUT 21st Century Publishing and Communications, Inc.

A Haights Cross Communications Company

http://www.chelseahouse.com

First Printing

1 3 5 7 9 8 6 4 2

Library of Congress Cataloging-in-Publication Data

Dendinger, Roger.
   Costa Rica / by Roger Dendinger.
      p. cm.—(Modern world nations)
Includes bibliographical references and index.
Contents: Introducing Costa Rica—Natural landscapes—Costa Rica through time—
People and culture—Government—Economy—Regional contrasts—Costa Rica
looks ahead.
   ISBN 0-7910-7242-8
   1. Costa Rica—Juvenile literature. [1. Costa Rica.] I. Title. II. Series.
F1543.2 .D46 2002
972.86—dc21

                                                            2002015800

Table of Contents

MODERN WORLD NATIONS

Costa Rica

Tortuguero National Park has beaches where marine turtles have traditionally nested for many years. Costa Rica's national park system is the pride of its people and is regarded as one of the finest in the world. The availability of land and the vision of a future that would preserve plant and animal diversity came together in the l970s in plans for this park system.

Introducing Costa Rica

I n a region of violent physical and cultural contrasts, Costa Rica is often easy to overlook. Among the six small countries of Central America, it tends not to make the news very often. Costa Rica is *not* the Central American country with the famous U.S.-built canal and the corrupt military dictator overthrown by U.S. armed forces in 1991. It is *not* the one ruled by Marxists for most of the 1980s and with whom the U.S. waged a small proxy war. It is *not* the one that suffered through nearly 35 years of a civil war that has only recently ended.

The natural disasters associated with Central America—hurricanes, earthquakes, volcanic eruptions—also seem to happen elsewhere in the region, just across the border in Nicaragua or to the south in Panama. In 2000, Hurricane Mitch, for example, killed thousands of people in Central America and devastated much of the banana industry in Guatemala, Honduras, and Nicaragua, but it spared Costa Rica.

Is Costa Rica lucky? In part, this may be the case. Major tropical storms and hurricanes in the Caribbean Basin usually strike just to the north of Costa Rica. The country's history certainly reveals some lucky decision-making. For instance, the first Spanish colonists avoided settlement close to the country's active volcanoes; this was not the case in other parts of the region. It is also true that Costa Rica has worked to avoid the mistakes made by its neighbors.

While international attention has focused on the plight and misery of its neighbors, Costa Rica has quietly worked to develop democratic institutions and a sense of national identity that makes it exceptional, not just in the context of Central America but throughout the world. As the civil wars and political problems of the region seem to be coming to an end in the twenty-first century (due in part to efforts that began in Costa Rica), the country is emerging from the shadow of its violent neighbors. The world is finally recognizing Costa Rica as a natural wonderland and as a political model for stability and peace.

LUCK AND VISION IN CENTRAL AMERICA

One of the themes of this book is Costa Rica's "exceptionalism," the ways in which it is different from its neighbors. Costa Rica will be compared and contrasted with the rest of Central America to understand this difference. What separates the country from its neighbors is a combination of luck and vision.

To have luck, or to be lucky, is to obtain success by chance. In its regional context, Costa Rica has indeed been lucky. That is, many of the country's qualities today grew out of circumstances that seemed unimportant or even disadvantageous in the past. Today, some of these same circumstances of geography and history seem fortunate as shown by the following examples.

For the first three hundred years of its settlement by Europeans, Costa Rica was an out-of-the-way place in the

Spanish New World. The conquistadors and missionaries who explored and settled the Americas ignored that part of the isthmus that came to be called Costa Rica "the Rich Coast." Despite its name, it had no gold nor silver; no great Amerindian tribes lived there. The large Spanish land grants made to minor nobles or conquistadors were almost all made elsewhere. The lack of a sizable Indian population was seen as a disadvantage to colonial administrators looking for labor on the haciendas, the cattle ranches, and the mines that they were establishing in Mexico and other parts of the empire. Early settlers in Costa Rica were small farmers, not the kind of grand colonizers Spain was hoping to attract.

Just to the south, Panama quickly became important as a land route across the isthmus, linking the Atlantic and the Pacific Oceans. Panama was placed under the control of the wealthy Spanish administrative center in Bogotá. Close by, but separated from Panama by thick steaming rain forest, tangled jungles, and rugged mountains, Costa Rica became part of another colonial governance system. It lay at the southernmost end of the Viceroyalty of New Spain, a large territory centered on Mexico City that extended from North America to the Talamanca Mountains along the Panamanian border. For centuries, Costa Rica was perceived as an unimportant wilderness, a place unlucky in its location and its settlement.

Today, however, the lack of a large Indian population is rather lucky in contrast to what has happened in other parts of Central America. Class-based divisions grew up in all of the other countries that developed large populations of mixed-blood people. These mixed-bloods, or *mestizos*, have suffered centuries of repression and discrimination throughout Latin America. The Indian people in places such as Guatemala have also been officially discriminated against; at times in the recent past military dictatorships made them second-class citizens in their own countries.

The political values and systems that grew up around these social divisions are still serious problems in Guatemala, El

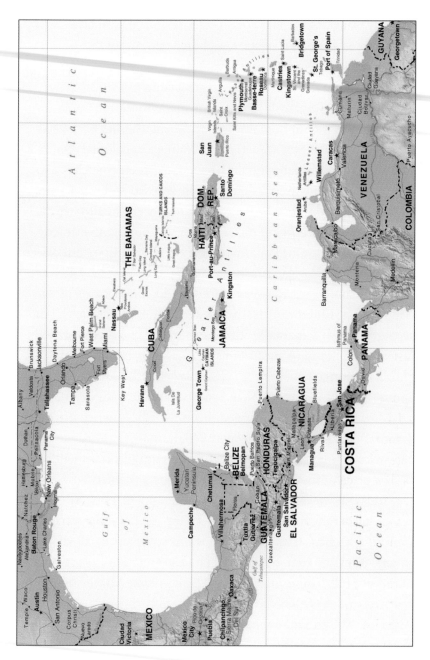

Between Mexico and South America lies a collection of small countries known as Central America. Guatemala, El Salvador, Honduras, Nicaragua, and Costa Rica were governed as a unit under Spanish rule and only became separate republics in 1838–39.

Salvador, and other countries. Costa Rica certainly has class divisions, as almost all societies do, but they are muted by a sense of national unity lacking in other Central American states. No revolutionary forces hide in the mountains. Ethnic politics do not polarize the people.

Luck has been important, but on the other hand, vision—intelligent foresight—has also shaped the country. Costa Rica's progressive social values have been nurtured carefully by generations of politicians and civic leaders. These democratic values are enshrined in the 1948 constitution. Currently, a long-range vision of the country as a place of economic expansion and growing wealth motivates Costa Rica's leaders to support free trade. According to this vision, the short-term adjustments necessary to open the economy to global trade may be painful for some, but future gains will benefit the country as a whole.

Sometimes, luck and vision come together. The story of Costa Rica's magnificent National Park system is an example. Each of the six Central American countries contains rugged mountains and tropical seashores, emerald rain forests, and cool highlands. Only Costa Rica had the vision to preserve some of its natural bounty for the future. When the idea of setting aside large tracts of undeveloped land for a system of parks and wildlife reserves was proposed in the 1970s, there was almost no political opposition. Historically, settlement had been concentrated in the temperate coffee-producing lands of the central highlands. There was no serious settlement pressure elsewhere in the country. The land seemed big enough to accommodate the preservationist vision. As a result, Costa Rica's park system is regarded as one of the finest in the world today.

With its Central American neighbors, Costa Rica shares a language, a religion, and a colonial history. It shares a similar physical geography as well. As shall be seen, Costa Ricans have made something very different out of these common cultural materials and physical characteristics.

Tourists visiting Poás National Park can look into the main crater of the Poás Volcano. Costa Rica has 7 active and nearly 60 extinct or dormant volcanoes. This park lies 37 miles (60 kilometers) northwest of the capital city of San José.

CHAPTER

2

Natural Landscapes

I n a region long associated with military coups and dictatorships, Costa Rica is known as the "Switzerland" of Central America. It is a political bridge linking North American-style democracy and Latin American cultural traditions. In physical terms, it is a land bridge for plants and animals moving through the Central American isthmus. Formed in the late Pliocene epoch (about 2.5 to 3 million years ago) by a shift in the Caribbean tectonic plate, the isthmus linked the two great landmasses of the Western Hemisphere at a crucial time in evolutionary development.

This was the epoch that saw the "modernization of mammals," and the development of polar ice caps, as well as the joining of the Americas. The term for the movement of plants and animals north and south over this narrow bridge is the Great American Interchange. In places only 80 miles (129 kilometers) wide, the

Central American or Meso-American land bridge acted as a biological filter for this interchange, selecting some species for passage and acting as a barrier to others. Many North American species (cats, dogs, bears) moved south; relatively fewer South American creatures moved north. Successful migrants to the north included armadillos, porcupines, opossums, and the now extinct giant ground sloth.

The unique tropical setting of this midway point between North and South American biological realms is now world famous for its commitment to preservation of its rich natural heritage. Proportionally, Costa Rica protects more of its national territory than any other country in the world.

Extending from eight to eleven degrees north latitude, Costa Rica lies entirely within the tropics, but elevation and rainfall vary greatly within the country. This close to the equator, the length of daylight does not vary much through-out the year. Nevertheless, dramatic differences in local, or micro, climates, make it difficult to generalize about the country's weather. Within an area slightly larger than the state of West Virginia, Costa Rica's natural landscapes range from exotic emerald green forests in the northeast, where heavy rains are constant year-round, to cold mountain peaks in the south-central region, and to seasonally dry grasslands in the rain shadow of the Nicoya Peninsula on the northwest Pacific coast.

Added to this diversity of landscapes is the fact that the geologically active Ring of Fire touches Costa Rica. The country has 7 active and nearly 60 extinct or dormant volcanoes. Several are among the most perfectly shaped composite volcanoes, or stratovolcanoes, in the world.

The natural hazard posed by volcanism throughout Central America is the result of the collision of lithospheric plates. These plates are giant pieces of Earth's outer shell that ride the surface of the planet, sometimes grinding against one another, sometimes pulling apart, and sometimes crashing head on in a continuous, extremely slow-motion action (very slow in human terms). When one plate is composed of denser material than another, a process known as subduction occurs. In the western waters off Central America, the thin and dense Cocos plate collides with the thicker continental Caribbean plate and is slowly being pushed down. As the Cocos plate descends, some of its material melts and rises to the surface as magma.

The resulting chain of volcanic mountains in Central America lies roughly parallel to the line of the Cocos plate's descent under the Caribbean plate. Costa Rica's stratovolcanoes are steep-sided structures, built from layers of ash and lava, and topped by bowl-shaped summit craters. Four of the most prominent—Poás at 9,055 feet (2,760 meters), Barba at 9,612 feet (2,930 meters), Irazú at 11,417 feet (3,480 meters) and Turrialba at 11,220 feet (3,420 meters)—sit in the middle of the country, not far from the heavily populated Central Valley region.

Earthquakes are related natural hazards in Costa Rica. Worldwide, quakes occur near plate subduction zones. Pressure from subduction is occasionally released when fault lines along plate boundaries slip suddenly. In Costa Rica the effects of such slippage can be severe. The April 22, 1991, earthquake measured 7.4 on the Richter scale.

CLIMATE

Winter as experienced in most of North America is nonexistent in Costa Rica, but some subregions of the country have cool, even cold weather. Here, as in much of the rest of Central America, temperature is modified by elevation rather than seasonal shifts in the sun's angle. Altitudinal zones are measured slightly differently from region to region in Central and South America. However, the elevation boundaries are much the same and the same names are applied to these zones, from Mexico to Brazil.

Before looking at the altitudinal zones in detail, the world climate classifications as applied to Costa Rica should be mentioned. Tropical climates are winterless with the coolest average monthly temperature warmer than 64°F (18°C). Tropical climates are also described by variations in rainfall that depend on prevailing winds, elevation, and ocean currents.

More than half the country, the half lying to the east of the Continental Divide, is classed as a wet tropical, or tropical rainforest, climate. This subregion receives more than 2.5 inches (6.35 centimeters) of precipitation each month of the year. The western third is a wet-and-dry tropical climate; it is hot all year and marked by a seasonal difference in rainfall. Summer months tend to be wet and the winter relatively dry on average. Located on the boundary between the wet tropical and wet-and-dry tropical types, Costa Rica's national capital, San José, receives an average of 8 to 13 inches (20 to 33 centimeters) of rain a month between May and October. Between December and April, the monthly average drops to between 0.5 to 2 inches (1.27 to 5 centimeters).

ALTITUDINAL ZONES

To make sense of the variety of local physical conditions in Costa Rica, understanding topography, the shape of the natural landscape in terms of its relief, or differences in elevation, is necessary. Geographers define variations in tropical subregions by the physical characteristics determined by elevation. Altitudinal zonation is a way to understand local variations in temperature, humidity, and vegetation that characterize much of Central America. The four zones are *tierra caliente, tierra templada, tierra fria,* and *tierra helado.* In higher elevations of South America's Andes Mountains, a fifth zone, the *tierra nevado,* is designated.

The tierra caliente (literally, "hot earth," or "hot land") extends from sea level upward to 2,500 feet (762 meters). In these lowland areas, ample year-round sunlight and humidity create a consistently warm, and usually very wet, environment. Plantation agriculture is often found in this zone. As in other parts of Central America, banana and sugar cane plantations are found in the lowlands, especially on the Caribbean coast. In the tierra templada ("tempered land") at 2,500 to 6,000 feet (762 to 1,829 meters), temperatures are more moderate. Although still warm, the templada has somewhat cooler temperatures at night. At this altitude, wheat and corn production occur throughout the region, but the signature crop of the templada is coffee. Coffee thrives in areas of volcanic soils and mild dry seasons. Approximately 247,000 acres (100,000 hectares) in Costa Rica are devoted to Arabica coffee, almost all of it in the Meseta Central, the Central Valley, and the surrounding mountains.

The tierra fria ("cold land") extends up to the tree line in the mountains, about 12,000 feet (3,600 meters). Beyond this point trees cannot grow in the rocky soils and cool year-round temperatures. Below tree line down to about 6,000 feet (1,829 meters), potatoes, barley, and dairying are common.

Above tree line, lies the tierra helado ("frozen land"). At 12,000 feet (3,658 meters) and up this area contains year-round snow and ice and poor, unconsolidated mountain soils. In portions of highland South America, the tierra helado is used seasonally for grazing, but Costa Rica has only a tiny bit of land lying in this uppermost altitudinal zone.

NATURAL REGIONS

Costa Rica sits on either side of the great mountain backbone of the Western hemisphere that runs along the Pacific side of the continent from Alaska to the tip of Tierra del Fuego. This mountain backbone is the Continental Divide of the isthmus. In Costa Rica, the mountainous region extends from northwest to southeast, dividing the country into two unequal coastal regions, the broken Pacific lowlands and the much larger Caribbean lowlands.

Within the mountainous region, higher elevations occur in the southern ranges known as the Cordillera de Talamanca. The Talamanca is home to Cerro Chirrip, the highest peak in the country at 12,533 feet (3,820 meters). The northern ranges, the Cordillera de Guanacaste, extend north into Nicaragua. Between Talamanca and the central volcanic ranges sits the Meseta Central, the Central Valley of Costa Rica, which is divided into the two intermountain basins of Cartago and San José. The Meseta Central extends approximately 40 by 50 miles (65 by 80 kilometers) within the tierra templada. With its somewhat cooler climate and well-drained volcanic soils, it has attracted settlers since Costa Rica's founding. Today it is heavily populated; almost two-thirds of the country's 3.7 million people live there. With a mild dry season, this is also the country's prime coffee district.

Coffee plants thrive at elevations ranging from about 2,500 to 5,000 feet (762 to 1,524 meters), and the first plants introduced by German settlers in 1790 grew luxuriantly. By the 1830s, coffee was grown throughout the Central Valley and the surrounding mountains. The first exports were to Columbia in 1820. In 1823 Costa Rican coffee was exported to Chile where it was repackaged under a Chilean name and shipped to Great Britain. A few years later, growers were selling directly to London. Production expanded throughout the nineteenth century and in 1890, access to the Atlantic coast from the Central Valley was completed, and exports to Europe began to leave from the Caribbean coast.

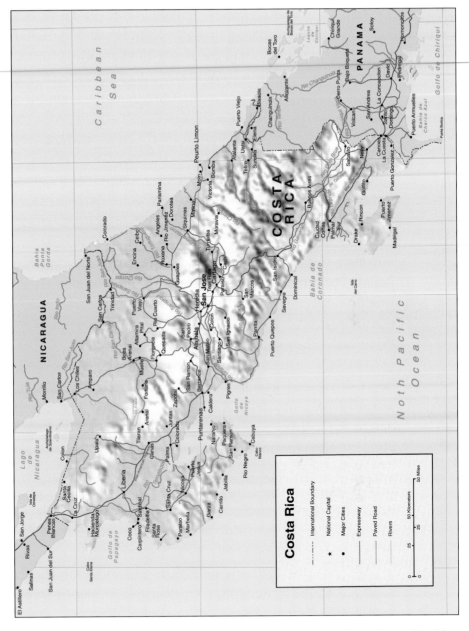

Costa Rica straddles the great mountain backbone that runs along the Pacific side of the Western Hemisphere. That "backbone," or Continental Divide, creates two unequal coastal regions—the Pacific lowlands and the much larger Caribbean lowlands. The half of the country that lies to the east of the divide is classed as a tropical rainforest climate.

Today, the Central Valley annually produces 2.6 million sacks of coffee, each weighing 132 pounds (60 kilograms). In the 1980s, coffee, long the staple of the national economy, slipped into second place in terms of export earnings. Bananas, grown primarily in the Caribbean lowlands, now make almost twice as much money as coffee. This is due in part to a depressed international coffee market and increased competition on the world market from newer coffee exporting countries such as Vietnam. Another factor is that banana plantations have been expanding since the 1980s.

The second region, the Pacific lowlands, is easily separated into two subregions: the northwest Pacific and southeast Pacific. They are separated by low mountain ranges that extend west from the continental divide. Two major peninsulas anchor the subregions: Nicoya Peninsula in the north and Osa Peninsula in the south.

The area around the head of the Gulf of Nicoya is the larger of the two, extending almost to Nicaragua. Here, the seasonally wet-and-dry tropical climate type is predominant due to the dry Pacific winds. A dry winter season creates a different vegetation regime. Here, rain forests border semideciduous forests and savanna-like grasslands. This northwest coastal region is also home to Costa Rica's rapidly growing cattle industry, especially in the interior portions of Guanacaste. Since the 1940s, land has been cleared for cattle and banana operations.

In the southeast Pacific subregion, where the Rio Diquis flows out of the mountains, a smaller area of coastal forest extends into Panama. From north to south, the Pacific coastline of the country is highly indented, in contrast to the straight Caribbean coastline.

The Pacific region is also known for its mangrove swamps. Mangrove landscapes are formed by halophytic (salt-tolerant) plants growing in sediments that accumulate along shorelines. Anchoring various plant species, mangrove roots are often visible above the water line; their thick root assemblages provide micro-niches for dozens of specialized plant, bird, and fish species. Over time, mangrove assemblages can retain enough material to form the basis for islands. Several mangrove areas along the coast are now protected as natural and wildlife preserves.

Costa Rica's third region is the Caribbean lowland. Extending south from Nicaragua's Mosquito Coast, this low, wet coastal plain receives some of the heaviest rainfall, 200 inches a year (508 centimeters), due to the prevailing Northeast trade winds. The wet heat of Costa Rica's east produces the densely tiered canopies of vine-draped equatorial rain forest for which the country is famous. Puerto Limón is the only good harbor on the Caribbean coast, which lacks the natural bays of the Pacific shore. The San Juan River marks the northern boundary with Nicaragua on the eastern side of the continental divide. This is banana country, although some banana operations have moved to the Pacific over the last few years as production has increased.

TROPICAL RAIN FOREST

Tropical rain forests, also known as equatorial forests, occur worldwide between the Tropics of Capricorn and Cancer. In these low latitudes, temperatures are high year-round, and rainfall is abundant. The resulting tropical evergreen forests contain the most diverse plant and animal communities in the world. Generally, the number of species increases as one moves from high latitudes to the equator. This is known as the diversity gradient and can be explained in part by the year-round abundance of solar energy found in low latitudes.

Unlike the popular image of thick jungle rain forests derived from Hollywood films, equatorial forests have little

A stream runs through the lush ferns, trees, and other plants in a tropical rain forest in Braulio Carrillo National Park. Contrary to their image as impenetrable jungles, rain forests have little undergrowth and are typically easy to walk through. Costa Rica's forests support a great diversity of plant and animal life.

undergrowth—it is possible to stroll through most rain forest regions without resorting to a machete (a long, heavy-bladed knife carried by many male residents of tropical lands). Life here is somewhat upside-down; the distribution of plant and animal life is vertical! Biogeographers estimate that only about one percent of available sunlight reaches the forest floor, so only plants that have adapted to survive in limited light grow there. High-level forest canopy (the upper levels of the tallest trees and their communities of air plants, climbing vines, tree-dwelling mammals, and birds) can top out at 200 feet (61 meters). Most of the biomass and nutrients of a tropical forest are thus suspended far overhead. By comparison, the lower-level forest floor is open and almost always in deep shadow.

Among the plant adaptations to this topsy-turvy world are epiphytes, the famous air plants of equatorial climates. Non-parasitic, although they grow on other plants, epiphytes survive entirely through photosynthesis. Another plant adapted to compete for sunlight in a vertically integrated ecosystem is the liana, or woody vine. Lianas root in the thin rainforest soil and quickly grow upward into the canopy. Reaching diameters of 8 inches (20 centimeters), lianas support air plants, orchids, and a host of bird and mammal life high over the forest floor, creating a "draped" effect in the upper canopy vegetation.

Both in and out of the rainforest ecosystem, Costa Rica's plant variety is staggering. Dozens of varieties of orchids grow in three of Costa Rica's four altitudinal zones. Over 2,000 species of bromeliads, a family that includes pineapples and Spanish moss, live throughout the forested regions while hundreds of moss, fern, and lichen species add a burnished color to the forest's palette.

DEFORESTATION

Despite the vast diversity of life forms they support, rain-forest soils, or oxisols, are thin and nutrient-poor. High heat and rainfall leach minerals from these soils, which tend to be reddish or yellowish due to the high amount of iron and aluminum oxides left behind. Oxisols are prone to a process known as laterization if they are exposed to the direct and intense sunlight of the tropics. The result of laterization, or hardening of the soil, is a substance called plinthite or laterite, which is so durable it is sometimes cut into bricks and used as building material. Hardening of the soil slows or even stops the process of forest rejuvenation.

As in other tropical regions around the world, Costa Rica's rain forests are threatened by deforestation and the long-term problems associated with laterization. One source of deforestation is the traditional agricultural practice known as "slash and burn," a shifting, land-intensive type of subsistence farming that destroys rain forests in Central and South America, Africa, and Southeast Asia.

In tropical slash and burn, a farmer clears a plot of rain forest, usually 3 to 5 acres (1.2 to 2 hectares), which is the maximum area a subsistence family can handle. All of the cleared vegetation is burned on site. Burning fixes nitrogen and other minerals in the soil, temporarily boosting soil fertility. Crops such as manioc and yams are planted. In the warm, wet low latitudes, farmers can produce up to three crops a year, so the plot is usually worked year-round without a fallow (idle) period. After three to six years, the beneficial effects of the burning wear off. Productivity declines, the plot is abandoned, the subsistence family looks for another piece of forest, and the cycle begins again. Cattle ranchers often take up abandoned rainforest land. Grazing cattle strip the fragile landscape of what little vegetative cover it might have, and serious erosion problems develop. If the soil is directly exposed to high heat and moisture, laterite forms.

Throughout history, traditional subsistence practices were not a problem; human populations were low, land was

Traditional slash and burn agriculture is destroying rain forests in many parts of the world, including Costa Rica. Here, bean plants cover an area that has been cleared and burned for agricultural use. This technique has been used for hundreds of years, but growing populations in the tropics are threatening to consume the Earth's remaining rain forests.

abundant, and abandoned subsistence plots had time—often a century or more—to recover. For the past hundred years however, populations in the tropics have been steadily growing. Now, in the twenty-first century, subsistence agriculture threatens to consume Earth's remaining rain forests. The

United Nations Food and Agriculture Organization estimates that approximately 0.6 percent of Earth's rain forests are lost each year to deforestation. Another sobering estimate is that half of Earth's rain forests have been cut down in the past 50 years. Central America has lost about 85 percent of its rainforest area since the middle of the twentieth century when deforestation began accelerating.

Subsistence farming is not the only threat, of course. As Costa Rica becomes a significant exporter of cattle for the U.S. market, clearing land for cattle ranching is a new reason for deforestation. Rain forests, sometimes called the "Earth's lungs," are important to world climate. Tropical rain forests help clean the atmosphere; 2.5 acres, (1 hectare) of healthy rain forest produces about 172 pounds (78 kilograms) of oxygen every day.

ANIMALS

A roll call of Costa Rica's animal life encompasses some of the most exotic names in the animal kingdom. These names exemplify the mystery, danger, and romance of the tropics: jaguars, tree sloths, peccaries, tapirs, agoutis, pacas, coatis, kinkajous, and margays. The list of names is a long one because the biological heritage of Costa Rica is complex and dazzling. Approximately five percent of the total number of species living on Earth resides within the country's national borders. Some animals are well known to environmentalists. For example, four types of marine turtles nest on the country's Pacific Coast beaches, including the leatherback, which, weighing nearly a ton, is the world's largest sea turtle. The elaborate web of life in Costa Rica's tropics also contains tens of thousands of little known insect, bird, and plant species.

Costa Rica's exotic animals include crocodiles, which live along both Pacific and Caribbean coasts, speckled caimans, and four species of New World monkey (the capuchin, howler, spider, and squirrel monkeys). Creatures that are only now being discovered and studied by scientists, such as the poison dart, or poison arrow, frogs, are common in many parts of the equatorial forest. Costa Rica's poison dart frogs produce some of the most powerful toxins in the animal kingdom; one species can even squirt a poisonous spray at potential predators! Other exotics include poison sea snakes and almost one hundred species of bats, one of which sports a two-foot wingspan and catches fish using sonar.

Four types of coral snakes highlight Costa Rica's gallery of toxic creatures. There is a tropical rattlesnake more deadly than its North American cousins. The infamous fer-de-lance, a member of the pit viper family of poison snakes, grows up to 6.5 feet (2 meters) long. Its venom is extremely toxic, and even a baby fer-de-lance packs enough poison to kill an adult human. Well camouflaged, it is an ambush predator, blending into a variety of environments and living without fear of people or natural predators.

In total, about 135 snake species live in Costa Rica, including several types of boa constrictor. Non-poisonous, and generally not a threat to humans, boas are carnivorous, killing their prey by squeezing or constricting. Boas grow continuously throughout their lifetime and average 6 to 10 feet (2 to 3.5 meters) in length and weigh over 65 pounds (29 kilograms), although much larger individuals have been recorded. Very well camouflaged, boas prey on small and even medium-sized mammals.

Benign, but just as exotic as the large animals, are the 1,000 species of butterflies and at least 630 resident species of birds (including brilliantly-colored toucans, macaws, and 51 types of hummingbirds). On the forest floor, army and leaf-cutting ants, in colonies composed of millions of individuals, are preyed upon by two types of anteaters.

The resplendent quetzal has been treasured in the Central American region since ancient times. This photograph was taken in the Monteverde Cloud Forest Reserve in Costa Rica, which is run by a private, not-for-profit organization. Quetzals can also be found in at least four of the country's national parks in the nation.

Perhaps the most sought after creature among ornithologists, photographers, and bird watchers is the resplendent quetzal. This relatively rare green and red bird is small in stature but sports iridescent green tail feathers up to 24 inches

(61 centimeters) long. In flight, these feathers undulate gracefully behind the bird's compact body and tufted head. Ancient Mayans and Aztecs worshipped a god, Quetzalcóatl, the Plumed Serpent, who wore a headdress of quetzal feathers. Mayans made killing the bird a capital offense!

Still held in esteem by the descendents of the Mayans, quetzals are today the national symbol of Guatemala. Naturalists report, however, that populations of this revered bird are much higher in Costa Rica, where deforestation has not destroyed as much of its cloud forest habitat as in other parts of Central America. The quetzal is found in at least four of Costa Rica's national parks, which afford protection for this and many other rare and threatened species. Costa Rica's political commitment to conservation and preservation of its natural landscapes is a success story for environmental science and serves as a model for other developing countries in the tropics.

NATIONAL PARKS AND CONSERVATION

Costa Rica is justly proud of its record as a frontline state in the fight to preserve biodiversity. As an international destination for "ecotourists," the country has devoted increasing amounts of government and private resources to protecting unique ecosystems and endangered species. European and North American scientists, international non-governmental environmental organizations, and agencies such as the World Bank and the United Nations have all created a global clientele for the environment in Costa Rica. Because of the fragile nature of tropical ecosystems and developmental pressures from the tourist industry, plantation agriculture, and cattle ranching, a shift from purely governmental to private efforts is underway.

With a $34 million loan from the World Bank in 2000, Costa Rica's Fondo Nacional de Financiamiento Forestal, or National Forestry Financing Fund, provides money to small landowners for forest conservation and small-scale reforestation projects. Critical areas adjacent to existing national parks and wildlife refuges are targeted as needing special attention. Improving water quality around protected areas is another targeted goal. At the global scale, this private-public partnership seeks to maintain Costa Rica's impressive carbon sequestration levels by preserving the health of the equatorial forests.

The Forestry Fund and other smaller projects under-taken in the country reflect the latest rainforest research conducted by conservation biologists. As these scientists learn about the complex interactions in tropical biomes (all life in a single, geographic ecosystem), they have come to understand a simple fact: as patches of equatorial forest (or any other forest type for that matter) become isolated, plant and animal biodiversity, as well as other indicators of forest health, decline. It is now widely under-stood that preserved natural areas require contact with other relatively undisturbed areas if they are to remain healthy. "Forest corridors," or biological superhighways are now being created to link the national parks and wildlife refuges in Costa Rica.

Beyond the national level, the forest corridor idea is influencing regional planning throughout Central America. Regional Conservation Units (RCUs) are the centerpiece for new, coordinated international efforts to preserve rainforest diversity. The most ambitious and impressive use of the RCU concept is the Paseo Pantera, the Path of the Panther, a project that will create a continuous conservation area along the Caribbean coast from southern Mexico and Belize south to Costa Rica and Panama. With the Central American panther as the symbol of the project, the Paseo Pantera is generating a new round of international support for rain-forest conservation. A welcomed side benefit of the plan is increased political cooperation among the sometimes quarrel-some Central American community.

Costa Rica has been a pioneer in transborder environmental protection. The country's transboundary La Amistad (Friendship Park) Biosphere Reserve unites one of the country's largest portions of undisturbed rain forest in a remote portion of Costa Rica's southeast with a preserved forest area across the border in Panama. In the north, the Sí-a-Paz ("Yes to Peace") project will create an international park on both sides of the San Juan River, which separates Costa Rica and Nicaragua.

Within its national borders, Costa Rica has established a conservation framework, which identifies and protects representative environments and habitats. Almost 25 percent of the country is now protected, either as a national park, reserve, wildlife refuge, or bio-corridor linking larger preserves. Some of these designations extend protection to entire ecosystems. Others target local populations of threatened species or unusual topographic features, such as the limestone caves in Barra Honda National Park, or the Cahuita National Park, which was created to protect coral reefs off the Caribbean coast.

The range of protection is impressive, ranking with the conservation history of the United States in its biological breadth. Las Baulas Marine Park protects critically important nesting habitat of the giant leatherback turtles (known as *baulas*). Ostinal Wildlife Refuge protects habitat of Pacific Ridley sea turtles, whose *arribadas* ("arrivals") were traditionally times of great turtle decimation. Before being protected, sea turtle eggs were widely considered a delicacy along coastal areas, and even today may be found on the menus of some local restaurants. Tamarindo Wildlife Refuge protects a Pacific coast mangrove swamp. In the Gulf of Nicoya, Guayabo, Newgritos and Pajaros Islands Biological Reserve protects unpopulated islands that are used as nesting habitat by seabirds. Ballena Marine Park is almost entirely under water. Designed to protect marine resources, this watery refuge is seasonally home to migratory whales ("*ballena*" is Spanish for whale) and is the year-round home of spotted dolphins.

It is, however, in the establishment of its grand ecosystem preserves that Costa Rica has earned its reputation as a world leader in park and wild land conservation. Corcovado National Park is world famous among biologists for its extensive protection of rainforest biodiversity near the Osa Peninsula. Perhaps the most biologically diverse area in Central America, Corcovado contains an estimated 10,000 insect species, all six of Central America's cats, and large populations of scarlet macaws. Scientists have counted up to 100 tree species in 2.47 acres (1 hectare) of Corcovado. This remote corner of the country bears little imprint of human development, and portions of it are true wilderness. Closer to the human population concentrated in the Central Valley, Braulio Carrillo National Park encompasses another large rainforest area less than an hour's drive from the capital city of San José. Noted for its ornithological diversity, the Braulio Carrillo park is home to more than 400 resident bird species.

Not all big parks focus on rainforest protection. Guanacaste National Park in Costa Rica's northwestern corner conserves tropical dry forests, a unique type of equatorial forest much different from the famous emerald green rain forests of the Caribbean slope. Noted North American biologist David Janzen has identified the tropical dry forest as an endangered ecosystem worldwide, and he was instrumental in the creation of the Guanacaste Park in the 1980s.

Several other parks feature Central America's premier natural hazard. The showpiece of Arenal National Park is the Arenal volcano, which erupted dramatically in July 1968 after centuries of lying dormant. More than 80 people were killed by the sudden eruption, and Arenal is now in an active phase, periodically erupting in spectacular displays that awe nighttime tourists. Another park devoted to volcanism is Poás Volcano National Park. Poás boasts one of the widest active craters of any stratovolcano in the world, measuring almost a mile (1.5 kilometers) from edge to edge.

Becoming a model brings with it new responsibilities for Costa Rica's political leadership. As it succeeds in preserving its unique natural heritage, the country attracts increasing numbers of ecotourists, whose presence is both a boon to the national economy and a threat to the achievements of the past decade of conservation victories. Without increased scientific vigilance and governmental care, the estimated one million visitors a year may be "loving the parks to death."

There is evidence that the first humans arrived in Costa Rica more than 12,000 years ago. Adrian Badilla, archaeologist with the National Museum, speaks with students at the site of a burial ground in Curridabat, a town near San José. Archaeologists found 25 grave sites of people they believe were ancestors of a group of indigenous (native) people called the Guetare. These ancestors are believed to have lived in the Central Valley around 800 A.D.

3

Costa Rica Through Time

O ne of the world's great archeological mysteries lies scattered across the countryside of southwest Costa Rica. Solid rock spheres, most made of granite or andesite, stand alone next to roads or rest in the middle of fields. Others are grouped in simple alignments near ancient cemeteries. Some are mounted on cobble-stone beds. Although all 500 spheres have smooth-textured surfaces, no two are the same size. Some are about as big as basketballs; others are over 6.5 feet (2 meters) in diameter and weigh as much as 16 tons (14.5 metric tons). Many of them miss being perfectly spherical by only several inches.

Physical evidence suggests the rocks were transported from miles away to the Diquis River delta where most of them are found. The production technique of the people who made them is still unknown. No construction sites have been located, and no partially completed spheres have ever been found. No overall pattern of their placement has emerged. Scientists believe they may have been created between 200 and 300 A.D. Theories abound as to their precise origin and cultural meaning. Were they created over long stretches of time by generations of craftsmen, or did individual artisans create them? It will probably never be known.

What is known is that ancient Costa Rica was a place of interaction between Mayan and Aztec cultures and Andean groups to the south. Just as the Middle American isthmus blends the plants and animals of North and South America, it also bridged northern and southern Amerindian cultures. Scientists define this region as a cultural buffer zone. Over centuries of interaction, a unique cultural synthesis shaped the lives of the people there.

Sophisticated scientific tests indicate that people lived in this part of the land bridge at least 12,000 years ago, but almost nothing is known about those first inhabitants. Archeologists have determined that in about 2000 B.C., people lived in small farming villages. Some, such as the people in the northwest Guanacaste-Nicoya region, maintained regular trade networks with Mexico and Guatemala at least as early as 800 B.C. Jade, ceramic, and gold trade items from the north have been found in Guanacaste and in the central mountains. For unknown reasons, trade with the north slowed and eventually stopped around 500 A.D. What happened to disrupt this trade is another mystery. From this time until the coming of the Europeans, southern influence in the region grew.

What little is known of the people who inhabited the isthmus comes from the site of Guayabo, on the slopes of the Turrialba Volcano. Guayabo is the largest and most important archeological site in Costa Rica. At its height, as many as 10,000 people lived there, making it a major city by ancient standards. Scientists have uncovered paved sidewalks, aqueducts, and large ceremonial buildings that reflect both northern and southern cultural influences. Evidently, Guayabo reached its peak between 300 and 700 A.D. As in the case of the Anasazi settlements in North America and the Mayan cities of the Yucatan, Guayabo was abandoned suddenly and for unknown reasons. A few hundred years before the age of European exploration, the cultural profile of the isthmus changed dramatically.

COLUMBUS

One of the first Europeans to set foot in Costa Rica was 13-year-old Fernando Columbus, son of the famous explorer Christopher Columbus. Much of what is known about Columbus's exploration of the Caribbean coast of Central America comes from Fernando's biography of his famous father.

After three voyages to the New World, Columbus had not found what he had been searching for—a sea route to the Far East. The existence of what soon became known as the Pacific Ocean was still conjecture at this point in history. Columbus believed a passage existed through the American landmass by which he could reach the Indian Ocean. His plan then was to circumnavigate the earth, returning to Spain around the Cape of Good Hope. Dreaming of discovering this water passage, Columbus embarked from the Spanish port of Cádiz on May 11, 1502, on his fourth and last voyage to the New World. Believing he would sail to Arabic lands on his voyage around the world, he brought along several Arabic interpreters. His brother accompanied him as captain of one of the four ships that made up the expedition.

After stopping at Caribbean outposts for supplies, Columbus and his fleet made their way west until they reached the coast of Central America. Sailing against the prevailing winds was difficult, but Columbus persisted in moving southeast along the coast, believing the passage to be in this direction. Stopping occasionally to barter with native people, he made landfall several times along the coast of what later would be called Costa Rica.

Near what is today Puerto Limón he stopped on September 18, 1502, and briefly explored the sparsely inhabited coast. Exploration of the land or the people was not his goal. Still believing in a passage to the west, he continued south, going as far as the Gulf of Darién before turning back. Discouraged, he returned to Spain in 1504, still believing in a westward passage and dreaming of circumnavigation.

SPANISH AMERICA

The Spanish Empire in the New World was vast. It would be nearly another century before the authorities in Madrid realized how much land they had claimed in the Americas. So after Columbus's brief visit to the Caribbean coast, the region was overlooked for many years.

Spain's priorities during the seventeenth century were acquiring gold and silver and converting the Amerindian peoples to Christianity. Although the Davila expedition of 1522 named the land Costa Rica, the "Rich Coast," this was a misleading name for conquistadors searching for quick riches. Costa Rica had no rich mines such as the Spanish found in Mexico or South America, and the native population was small. By the dawn of the sixteenth century, an estimated 20,000 to 30,000 people lived in the region. European diseases such as smallpox and tuberculosis quickly decimated this small population, almost completely wiping out the tribes of the Central Valley. The survivors fled to the Talamanca Mountains in the south where their descendents live today. The only significant population remaining in Costa Rica was the Chorotegas in the Nicoya Peninsula.

With no gold for the conquistadors, and no Indians for the priests to convert, the region was of little interest to the Spanish. Settlement was sporadic for many years after Columbus's voyage. In 1522, an outpost was established at the Nicoya Peninsula, but this was soon abandoned due to the hostility of the Chorotegas. By then, the Spanish had their hands full defeating and converting the tribes to the north and south and then developing the gold and silver mines found in those territories. Costa Rica became a back-water of the empire.

The first serious attempt to establish permanent settle-ments began in 1562 with the arrival of Francisco Vasquez de Coronado, the famous explorer of what is now the Southwestern United States. Appointed governor of Costa Rica, he collected the few scattered Spanish settlers along the coast and brought them to the tierra templada of the Cartago Valley. Coronado realized that the temperate climate and good soils of the region made it a logical place to develop self-sufficient agricultural settlements. He founded the town of Cartago in 1563 and made it the capital of the province.

Throughout the highlands, the Indians had died from disease or fled, so the settlers worked the rich land them-selves. Even Coronado worked his own fields. Costa Rica was one of the only places in Spanish America where farming was practiced by Spanish settlers and by people of unmixed Spanish blood. The province did not attract many settlers, but those who came, came to farm, not to prospect for gold. From its earliest settlement, Costa Rica was a place of small, self-sufficient landowners. In the long run, this served the country's future well. The tradition of egalitarianism—a belief in human equality—was established early on and became a hallmark of Costa Rican society.

One exception to the farming settlements of the tierra templada was found in the northwest. Closest to the Spanish administrative center in Guatemala, this subregion of Costa Rica had the greatest colonial influence in the early years. Here, as in other portions of Spanish America, land was divided into large private estates and cattle ranches. This tradition of cattle ranching persists. In the twenty-first century, this area, Guanacaste, is the center of Costa Rica's growing cattle export industry. Another exception was the Caribbean coast. With no natural harbors, this eastern side of the country was almost completely unsettled for nearly two hundred years after Columbus landed there. In the 1600s, it became a refuge for smugglers and pirates preying on colonial gold shipments from Mexico and South America. Pirates became such a menace that Spain officially closed the Costa Rican coast for many years.

Throughout the seventeenth and eighteenth centuries, Costa Rica grew slowly, attracting those relatively few Spanish settlers who wanted to establish themselves as small farmers. Spain handed down an edict that colonial populations resettle near churches, and gradually towns took shape. Coronado's town of Cartago was destroyed in 1723 by the eruption of Irazú Volcano and was later rebuilt. San José was founded in 1737, and because of its situation in the Central Valley, it soon became the leading city of the province.

Spain's control over Central America waned throughout the eighteenth century. Competing with England and France for colonial power in the Caribbean and North America and preoccupied with deteriorating conditions at home, Spain allowed the region to slip from its grasp. Among all the provinces of the old Spanish Main, Costa Rica was best positioned to take advantage of independence.

INDEPENDENCE

Paradoxically, the aspects of Costa Rica that made it a colonial backwater worked to the country's long-term advantage. In a region still marked by ethnic and cultural conflict, it had several advantages over its neighbors. The ethnic homogeneity of the small farming landowners served as a basis for democratic values. The small Indian and mixed-blood population resulted in a lack of class-based problems. Costa Rica's physical isolation from large population centers fostered a spirit of self-sufficiency and independence. These features contributed to the gradual formation of an individualistic and peaceful society.

When Central American independence came in September 1821, it made little difference to most people in Costa Rica. After a brief civil war in 1823, Costa Rica joined with Mexico, Guatemala, El Salvador, Nicaragua, and Honduras to form the Central American Federation (CAF). From its founding, the CAF suffered from a lack of common goals and concerns. It was also hampered by a lack of transportation and communication linkages. With a vast area stretching from the Rio Grande in the north to the Gulf of Darien in the south, the CAF began to dissolve peacefully almost as soon as it formed. In 1838, the federation ceased to exist, and Costa Rica formally became independent.

In contrast to the other former members of the CAF, Costa Rica quickly began building an export economy. The country's first elected president, Juan Mora Fernandez, installed many of the elements that were to make the country a stable and relatively prosperous place. He expanded public education and established a judicial system. Perhaps most importantly for the country's future, he realized the significance of coffee as an export crop. He encouraged coffee cultivation by giving free land and coffee seedlings to new growers. The pattern of settlement in the tierra templada established by Coronado continued. Settlement also began moving out of the Central Valley as available land became occupied by small coffee growers. Settlers moved beyond the upper limits of the templada into the tierra fria, as well as downslope into the tierra caliente.

The expanding coffee economy spurred the development of roads out of the Central Valley to the small Pacific and Caribbean ports. Until 1846, the only way to transport coffee out of the Central Valley was over oxcart trails winding down from the hills to the port at Puntarenas. From there the

This woodcut illustration, done in 1880, shows Costa Rican workers picking ripe coffee berries. Coffee and bananas were the key agricultural products in building a strong export economy.

coffee was loaded on ocean-going vessels for shipment around Cape Horn to Europe. The obvious inefficiency of this route led the government to finance construction of roads to the new Caribbean port of Limón.

By 1850, Costa Rica was Europe's main coffee supplier. Most Costa Rican coffee at this time was repackaged in Chile before it rounded the Horn and thus entered the European market labeled as a product of Chile.

Coffee growers, the *cafetaleros,* dominated the ruling elite during this time. Rivalry between the leading coffee families led to a period of militarism, but unlike other Central American republics, Costa Rica's military rulers were progressive and promoted the establishment of democratic institutions. During struggles among the cafetaleros, General Tomas Guardia overthrew the government in April 1870. Although Guardia was a military ruler, he still represented Costa Rica's tolerant and egalitarian traditions. He abolished capital punishment and used government revenues for building roads. He amended the constitution, making primary education obligatory and free for both boys and girls.

Under Guardia's leadership, Costa Rica was set on a course that would stabilize the country's export economy and shape its twentieth-century identity as one of the world's leading coffee and banana producers. Guardia's vision was to eliminate the long, dangerous trip around the Horn and to increase the value of European exports. His government began planning a rail link between the Central Valley and the Atlantic coast. Eventually, shipping costs were cut in half by the new railroad and the development of the port at Limón.

In 1871, Guardia's government hired a U.S. company to build a railroad connecting San José with Puerto Limón. The man who became head of the project would play a major role in shaping Costa Rica and neighboring countries. Minor C. Keith was born in Brooklyn, New York, and started his career in the Texas cattle industry. In 1871, his uncle, who had built railroads in Peru, invited him to Costa Rica to work on the project. Accepting the challenge, Keith left for Central America with his two brothers.

Construction through the rain forest was more difficult than anyone had imagined. The tropical climate diseases made the hard physical labor almost impossible. Nearly 5,000 men, including Keith's uncle and both of his brothers, died during the construction. The railroad's deadly reputation made it hard to recruit workers in Central America, so the company brought Jamaicans in to do the work. Their descendents still live along the Caribbean coast. Keith also recruited convicts from the jails of New Orleans. Of the 700 he brought to Costa Rica, fewer than 100 survived. On one occasion, he brought a ship of Italian immigrants from Louisiana, but when they discovered the miserable working conditions, they rebelled and sailed back to New Orleans.

Laying tracks through the humid lower slopes of the mountains and out into the rain forest of the coastal plain was agonizingly slow. The first 70 miles of line took nine years to complete. In 1882 the Costa Rican government defaulted on its payments, forcing Keith to borrow over one million dollars to finish the project. As a money-raising scheme, he transplanted banana trees from Limón that he planted in 1873 to supplement the diet of his rail workers. Keith had the idea of transporting bananas along the new line to the port and then exporting them to the United States. The wide Caribbean coastal plain was ideal for banana production. The soils there were fertile, derived in part from volcanic ash washed out of the mountains. The heavy rainfall and hot, year-round sun were perfect for banana growth.

At this time, bananas were exotic items in the United States. Most North Americans had never eaten one. The first small shipment to New Orleans in 1878 created an immediate local demand that quickly grew into a regional, then a national, market for the tropical fruit. Soon the value of Keith's banana plantations surpassed the value of the rail line he had built for the coffee industry.

Keith founded the Tropical Trading and Transport Company to coordinate his banana business and to provide transportation for his increasing shipments to the United States through the port of New Orleans. He expanded his banana empire to Colombia and to what was at the time Columbia's northernmost province, Panama. By 1899, he

In the late 1800s, North American entrepreneur Minor C. Keith had the idea of shipping bananas along newly built railway lines in Costa Rica for export to the United States. By the time this photograph was taken in 1910, the nation was the world's largest producer of bananas.

dominated the banana business in Central America, but in that year with the bankruptcy of a New York brokerage, he lost his fortune. Traveling to Boston to meet with his major rival, the Boston Fruit Company, Keith proposed a merger, and the United Fruit Company (UFC) was founded in March 1899.

Keith's UFC banana empire flourished on the simple idea of supply and demand. North Americans quickly developed a taste for the exotic fruit, and Costa Rica's banana exports boomed, soon becoming as important as coffee to the national economy. In 1890, before his rail line was completed, Keith's company exported one million bunches of bananas from Puerto Limón. Ten years later, 3.5 million bunches sailed to New Orleans and New York. In 1907 over 10 million bunches were shipped north. By 1909 Costa Rica was the world's biggest banana producer.

As the United Fruit Company grew, Keith became a very influential and respected man in Costa Rica. In 1908, he completed a Guatemalan railroad, enabling the UFC to develop banana plantations in the Guatemalan lowlands. He married the daughter of a Costa Rican president and worked as a negotiator with European banks on behalf of his adopted country. He dreamed of building a railroad network connecting North and South America. For good reason, Keith was called the "uncrowned king of Central America." His investments in railroads and banana plantations had a deep influence on the region's society.

THE TWENTIETH CENTURY

Keith's transportation infrastructure fueled the continued growth of the agricultural export economy well into the twentieth century. By the 1930s, political tension began to develop between urban reformists and rural farming interests. Election corruption and fraud in the 1948 election led to an insurrection led by José Figueres. Known as "Don Pepe," Figueres led the country through what became known as the War of National Liberation. The conflict, by Central American standards, was short. In only 44 days the fighting was over.

After the war, Don Pepe led the Founding Junta of the Second Republic of Costa Rica. In keeping with the country's traditions of progressivism, he was a benign military ruler. Although he temporarily banned the press and the Communist Party, he introduced suffrage for women and full citizenship for Costa Rica's black population, which lived on the Caribbean coast. Perhaps most surprisingly, he revised the constitution to permanently abolish the army. He was also responsible for establishing a presidential term limit. After restoring stability to the country and bringing about his reforms, Don Pepe did as he promised at the start of the 18-month junta period. He stepped down as leader and turned the government over to the man who had won the 1948 election, Otilio Ulate. Don Pepe became Costa Rica's greatest democratic hero and later ran for office himself, serving two terms as president, 1953–1957 and 1970–1974. A revered national figure, he died on June 8, 1990.

A Costa Rican woman dances to the rhythm of a *comparsa* band during a traditional year-end carnival in San José. A comparsa is made up of a variety of instruments, and is usually accompanied by singers and trumpeters who parade along with dancers who wear extravagant costumes.

CHAPTER

4

People and Culture

ational identities in Central America are often hard to understand. For example, what it means to be a Guatemalan depends in large part on who is asked. Are you talking to a mixed-blood peasant, an urban ladino, or a Mayan Indian? Is the person a landowner or a seasonal plantation worker? A Guatemalan's ethnic background, job, and place of residence all shape his or her perception of citizenship. A similar variation in class attitude is found in El Salvador, Honduras, and Nicaragua. Costa Rica, however, is different. Here, almost everyone would agree that most citizens share a common national identity. When asked what it means to be Costa Rican, most would describe similar traits and values that knit together the people of the country.

Costa Ricans call themselves "*Ticos*." The name derives from the old colonial expression, "we are all *hermaniticos*" (little brothers).

Ticos are very aware of their unique political history and are rightly proud of their democratic nonviolent politics. Like U.S. citizens, they value their constitution and its guarantees of free speech and a free press. Education is widely respected and pursued. (Government support for education is higher per capita than anywhere else in Latin America.)

Another source of national pride is the lack of a standing army. Ticos will point out that unlike its neighbors, Costa Rica doesn't need an army to keep the country from falling apart. While other states still suffer from the effects of authoritarian military rule, Costa Rica's open society is built on political competition and tolerance.

Ticos are also very aware of their relative position in a world region beset with social and economic problems. They tend to credit their constitution and their generally astute political leaders for their relatively high standing in Latin America. A sense of national unity and a concern for social welfare also set the country apart. For example, Costa Rica has always invested heavily in social service guarantees for its citizens. Regardless of which political party is in control of the executive or legislative branches of government, this commitment remains high.

Initiatives such as the Program for Rural Health receive wide support from all of the country's political parties. That program established rural clinics specializing in nutrition education and preventive care. It is only one example of the results of a sense of shared national destiny. Almost ten percent of the gross national product is spent on health care. Not surprisingly, the country has the highest life expectancy in Latin America, not far behind Canada and about the same as that of the United States. For men, life expectancy stands now at 75 years, and for women the figure is an impressive 79.

QUALITY OF LIFE

According to the United Nations Human Development Report, Costa Rica has one of the highest standards of living in the Western Hemisphere, outside of Canada and the United States. The U.N. Human Development Index (HDI) combines economic policy analysis with population data such as life expectancy and level of educational attainment. The resulting numerical profile indicates the relative ranking of the world's countries in terms of overall quality of life. In the words of the U.N. report, the purpose of the index is to gauge "human well-being, not just economic trends." A low score on the HDI indicates a high quality of life and political stability.

For example, Sweden, one of the world's most prosperous places, has an HDI score of 10. At the other end of the spectrum, the world's poorest countries, such as Afghanistan, have scores well over 100. Costa Rica is far ahead of most of its Central American neighbors in the HDI ranking (Figure 1).

United Nations Human Development scores (2000)	
El Salvador	78
Guatemala	76
Mexico	42
Panama	38
Costa Rica	31

Figure 1.

By all standard demographic measures, Costa Rica is in good shape. Its infant mortality rate (the number of deaths per 1,000 births) is 13, compared to 45 for Guatemala, 42 for Honduras, and 40 for Nicaragua. Its death rate (annual number of deaths per 1,000 people) is 4, which is the lowest in Latin America (along with Mexico). The country's fertility rate (the average number of children a woman will have during her lifetime) has fallen to 2.4, one of the lowest in Latin America. It does not face the serious problems of rapid population growth typical of its regional neighbors. Its doubling time (the number of years it will take a country's population to double) is low in comparison to developed countries, but is still higher than most Latin American or Caribbean states.

Many aspects of cultural, political, and economic life affect fertility. In most places in the world, regardless of culture, fertility rates decline as professional and economic opportunities for women become available. In the case of Costa Rica, economic diversification, the tradition of progressive politics, and an open educational system are important to understanding the decline.

Another factor in the country's falling fertility rate is the changing attitude regarding the culture of *machismo*. Machismo may be described as the cult of male virility, or an exaggerated sense of masculinity. A "macho" man expresses positive personal values, such as courage and loyalty to friends, but machismo is based also on male domination of women. Sometimes a source of satire in the United States, machismo is still an important aspect of social life in many Latin American countries. It continues to shape gender roles and perceptions for both women and men. Machismo's female equivalent, *marianismo*, is also still alive in Latin American culture. From this traditional perspective, women are expected to serve husbands and male relatives and allow them to make most decisions.

Costa Rica is a country whose national motto could well be "moderation in all things." Ticos, not surprisingly, temper their macho attitudes with more contemporary and progressive views. Although extreme expressions of machismo can be found elsewhere in Latin America, the Costa Rican variety is generally inoffensive, and even invisible, to most outsiders.

More than 77 percent of the population is Roman Catholic, but by Central American standards the country is very secular. Again, the national trait of moderation may be used to describe religion's role in the national culture. The church has never dominated politics as it has in other countries in the region. The Catholic Church was responsible for much of Spain's most beautiful colonial architecture. Splendid examples of seventeenth- and eighteenth-century cathedrals, monasteries,

The Cathedral of Los Angeles, 30 miles east of San José, is one of the many beautiful churches, cathedrals, and monasteries built by the Catholic Church.

and nunneries can be found in the Central Valley. Most people are proud of this rich historical legacy that is so prominent on the cultural landscape. Ticos are generally a religious people, but they have a long tradition of separating church and state.

Similar to Western or Northern Europeans, they see religion as a private matter involving personal choice. Lately, a gradual change in the religious life of the country has begun. Over the last two decades, various U.S. evangelical groups have been active throughout Central America. Slowly, the number of Protestants is growing. Currently about 18 percent of Costa Rica's population is Protestant.

Most of the country's people live in or near the cities of the tierra templada. The highland capital city of San José, with a metropolitan population of over one million, is the largest urban area. Other major cities in the mountains are Alajuela (250,000 people) and Cartago (150,000). Coastal cities of Puntarenas on the Pacific (300,000) and Limón on the Atlantic (150,000) have grown in population since the end of World War II. About half of the national population lives in urban areas.

ETHNICITY

Another unique characteristic of Costa Rica's culture is the country's ethnic profile. Unlike the rest of Central America, most Ticos are of European descent. A small indigenous population meant that very little intermarriage occurred during the colonial period. The class divisions and violent ethnic politics of most other Latin American countries are absent. Many of the farming families today, small, medium, and large landowners, are direct descendents of the pureblood Spanish coffee growers of the 1820s and 1830s. In the coffee highlands there are also descendents of German immigrants who came in the mid-nineteenth century. The Germans and a few English who immigrated at about the same time came to dominate almost 40 percent of Costa Rica's coffee exports by the early twentieth century. The political and social value of this ethnic and economic continuity is significant.

The lack of any sizable Indian population during the colonial period also meant that there was no tradition of forced labor as there was in other parts of Spanish America. Most settlers were people willing to work the land themselves. The lack of a surplus labor force became an advantage by the nineteenth century when Central America's five republics began competing in the export trade. Wages were higher in Costa Rica than in neighboring countries and have remained the highest since. Working the coffee harvest carried no stigma as it did in El Salvador or Guatemala.

Historians of the coffee trade report that young middle-class Costa Ricans routinely worked at harvest time on the *fincas* (farms) of friends or relatives. The lower population pressure during the colonial period also meant that land was distributed more equally. The problem of landless mestizos and Indians that characterizes the politics of Guatemala and El Salvador are absent.

Although Costa Rica suffers from no deep class divisions or ethnic divisions, an uneven distribution of wealth is still a problem, as it is in most parts of the world. Almost one-fifth of the population lives in poverty. These impoverished "*marginados*" are declining in number as the country continues to diversify and develop its economy. Nevertheless, the illegal slums of the marginados are a blemish on the outskirts of San José and the other large cities. The elimination of slums (which are called "*tugurios*") is a priority in a country that prides itself on its commitment to provide basic social services to all its citizens. Many of the marginados are recent economic and political migrants from Nicaragua. Primarily landless mestizos and Mosquito Indians, they came south to escape the Contra War of the 1980s. About 40,000 live along the San Juan River, Costa Rica's border with Nicaragua, and in the Caribbean coastal lowlands.

Despite the high degree of cultural and ethnic homogeneity in Costa Rica, local variations in ethnic identity may be found. One example is along the Atlantic lowlands in a coastal region centered on Puerto Limón. Here the population is almost one-third black. Most of these people trace their ancestry to the thousands of Jamaicans brought to build the Atlantic Railroad by Minor Keith in the 1870s and 1880s. After the banana trade created an export boom, most of the railroad workers stayed to work the United Fruit Company banana plantations.

Their descendents still speak an English patois (dialect) similar to that of the English Caribbean. Making up a small percentage of the national population, about 3 percent, black Ticos today number about 40,000. Under a system of apartheid, they were confined to the Atlantic lowlands by law for many years. The reforms of the 1949 constitution, however, gave them full citizenship rights. Since then the black Ticos have migrated to other parts of the country and are entering the mainstream of Costa Rican society.

Another local or regional variation in ethnicity is found in Guanacaste. This province has the highest number of mestizos in all of Costa Rica. About half of the 250,000 people there are of mixed Spanish and Indian blood. This is a result of the persistence of the Chorotago people who resisted the Spanish for many years and who gradually merged with the colonial cattle ranchers and settlers who moved into the province in the late sixteenth century. In some ways, the culture of Guanacaste resembles that found in the countries to the north, particularly Nicaragua, more than it does the Central Valley.

INDIANS

The low number of Indians makes Costa Rica unique in Central America. Throughout Spain's New World Empire, intermarriage with Indians was common. Distinct mixed-blood populations developed. These populations, variously called *ladinos* in Guatemala and *mestizos* in most of the rest of the region, created an ethnic-based class system.

Costa Rica's indigenous peoples number only about 30,000 today. This is approximately the same number of Indians as were living in the region at the time of Spanish exploration. Most have been completely acculturated to mainstream Costa Rican lifestyles. Almost 10,000 members of the Bribri, Boruca, and Cabecar tribes live in or near the Talamanca Mountains in the southwest portion of the country. This was the historic refuge area after the coming of the Spanish settlers and the introduction of European diseases in the sixteenth century.

The most traditional of Costa Rica's tribes are the Guaymí, who live near the border with Panama and frequently cross into Panamanian territory to visit and trade with friends and relations. The Guaymí retain more traditional Amerindian culture traits than other native groups. Many Guaymí women still wear colorful costumes similar to those worn by the people of Guatemala. In part, their physical isolation in the sparsely populated mountains has protected their old ways from change.

A Guaymí Indian girl picks coffee on a plantation near San Vito. The Guaymí are a traditional Indian tribe in Costa Rica, and many of them live in the southern part of the country near the border with Panama. Their isolated life in the mountains has allowed them to better retain their traditional ways.

The mountains serve as an environmental refuge protecting the language from rapid change. Nevertheless, the Guaymí and the other surviving tribal tongues are threatened with extinction. Each year, fewer young people learn the old languages.

In December 1977, the government passed a law establishing Indian reserves to help protect the tribes. In some important ways, the Costa Rican system of reserves resembles the U.S. system of Indian reservations. As in the United States, the government retains title to Indian lands, but the lands themselves are held for the exclusive use of tribal members. Tribal people who choose to live in the reserves have the right of limited self-government, much as North American tribes do on their reservation lands. Each family is allotted a 366-acre (148-hectare) land grant for farming. Non-Indians are prohibited from buying land within the reserves.

Fifteen of the 22 reserves lie southeast of the Central Valley. Because of the remoteness of many of these lands, the government has not always been successful in keeping out non-Indians who occasionally enter the reserves to harvest tropical hardwoods or search for minerals. However, the government is committed to protecting the tribal groups. Costa Rica's Indian people do not face the official persecution and informal discrimination that Indians in other parts of Latin America often do. In fact, the Talamanca tribes have made advancements that would be impressive even in the United States. Recently, Indian activists in the Talamanca area established the first indigenous bank in Central America.

Despite efforts to protect Indian identity, most younger Indians speak no native languages. Traditional religion and almost all of their material culture has also been forgotten. Costa Rica's tribes seem destined to follow the path of the Chorotegas. A well-established culture in the sixteenth century, they were gradually absorbed, genetically and culturally, into the hybrid society of the mestizo.

POPULAR CULTURE

Food in Costa Rica reflects the national trait of moderation. A first-time U.S. traveler through Mexico and Central America is likely to encounter two general types of cuisine, both somewhat extreme to North American tastes. The first type might be termed the hot and strange. The tradition of fiery peppers in Mexico is an acquired taste. The strange foods consist of local tastes and adaptations that are again, very exotic. Iguana, for instance, is occasionally eaten in Guatemala ("tastes like chicken"), and the eggs of endangered sea turtles are considered delicacies all along the Pacific coast.

The second general type is the bland food eaten daily by millions of peasants and subsistence farmers in the region. Tortillas, beans, eggs, and corn are the staples of their diet. This is a fairly nutritious diet, but the staple ingredients are prepared day after day without much variation.

By contrast, Costa Rica's cuisine tends to be somewhat exotic without falling into the category of strange or unappealing. Many native dishes, or "*comida tipica*," are based on combinations of black or pinto beans and rice. The national dish is g*allo pinto*, fried rice and black beans. Regional variations are common, such as Caribbean Rice and Beans (gallo pinto made with coconut milk). Another popular variation is *casado*, which is rice and beans served with cabbage and tomato salad, meat, and, occasionally, fried plantains. Costa Rica has no national drink as such, but *horchata*, a cinnamon-flavored cornmeal drink, is a traditional favorite. Coffee is popular everywhere. As in other Central American coffee-producing countries, however, most of the best beans are exported, so the quality is uneven. Coffee is traditionally served very strong and mixed with hot milk. Food staples include beef, especially in the northwest, and seafood along both coasts. American-style fast food is changing local tastes in the bigger cities.

Supporters of presidential candidate Abel Pacheco celebrate his lead in the election on Sunday, February 3, 2002. Costa Rica's elections have become a celebration of national politics and may even resemble a carnival day. Costa Ricans vote in higher numbers that do citizens of the United States, and election day is considered to be a time for waving flags and throwing confetti.

5

Government

"This is a country that dared to declare peace to the world." These words of French President Francois Mitterand identify the central political value that sets Costa Rica sharply apart from the rest of Central America. In this region of military dictatorships, civil wars, and brutal repression, Costa Rica's commitment to constitutional law and democracy is a twenty-first century example for all of Latin America.

More than just showing the way, Costa Rica has actively worked outside its borders to bring peace and economic growth to its neighbors. Its political nickname, the Switzerland of Central America, is well earned. As well as remaining neutral in regional and international disputes, it is becoming a world leader in conflict resolution. For such a small country, it has a very large reputation as a place committed to peaceful coexistence and nonviolent politics.

The story of Costa Rica's commitment to peace includes several exceptionally able leaders, such as Oscar Arias, but the real story is the tradition of constitutional law embedded in Costa Rica's political culture. The constitution establishes a governmental structure similar to that of the United States. The government is divided into three branches, an executive, headed by the president; a representative legislature; and a judicial branch.

The independence of the three branches of the national government is outlined in Article 9 that clearly expresses the idea of separation of powers. A fundamental concept in the U.S. constitutional structure, the separation of powers ensures that no branch of government can dominate the system.

The legislative branch is constitutionally designed to be strong, just as it is in the United States. The Legislative Assembly has the power to amend the president's budget and to oversee government spending by appointing a comptroller general. Also like the U.S. Congress, the Assembly can override presidential decisions by a two-thirds majority vote.

The right to declare war rests solely with the National Assembly, just as in the U.S. Congress. Legislators are thus powerful figures in the government. Known as *diputados* (deputies), they are elected to four-year terms, as is the president. A constitutional amendment, adopted in 1969, limits the president to one term in office, although an individual may serve again after one election cycle.

One difference between the Costa Rican system and the United States is that the legislative branch is unicameral, having just one legislative body as opposed to the American bicameral system of a senate and a house of representatives. Another more significant difference is that Costa Rica's democratic system is not federalist. In the United States, the government is thought of as consisting of layers. In fact, the U.S. system is sometimes described as "layer cake federalism." The national, or federal government, is the top layer, with the fifty states and thousands of county and city governments making up the second and third layers.

Costa Rica has no sharing of power from the top to the bottom layer, although it does have a subnational organization of seven provinces: Alajuela, Cartago, Guanacaste, Heredia, Limón, Puntarenas, and San José. A governor who is appointed by the president heads each province. The provinces might be thought of as the equivalent of the U.S. system of states, except for one important difference. The provinces have no legislatures of their own and thus do not make their own subnational laws. Their primary role in the system is to serve as electoral districts for the National Assembly. Provincial population determines the number of deputies from each province. One member is sent to the Assembly for each 30,000 people.

The seven provinces are further divided into 81 *cantones* (roughly equivalent to counties) that are subdivided into districts ruled by municipal councils. The districts and cantones have almost no power beyond that of insuring provision of basic public services such as garbage collection and road repair.

Another power invested in the Assembly is that of appointing judges to the Supreme Court. The judicial branch is traditionally respected as an independent guardian of the constitution, much as the U.S. Supreme Court is. Frequently, it acts to check both the president and the Assembly, and its rulings are accepted without much complaint. One of the constitutional duties of the court is to oversee elections which it does through a Special Electoral Tribunal.

In part because of the fair and conscientious work of the tribunal, election time in Costa Rica is "something of a fiesta," in the words of travel author Paul Theroux. In sharp contrast to the violence and corruption associated with elections in other Central American countries, Costa Rican elections are proud public displays of political tolerance and democratic decision-making. Elections are held on the first Sunday in February, a day that has become as much a celebration of national politics as it is an opportunity to choose representatives. People wave flags, throw confetti, and proudly hold up their thumbs, dyed purple at the voting stations, to show they voted. School children assist at the voting booths, lending an air of community involvement to the proceedings. Costa Ricans vote in high numbers, far more than the citizens of the United States. Like most other representative democracies, it is a country of universal suffrage. All citizens are automatically registered and issued a voting card on their eighteenth birthdays. Unlike the United States, voting is compulsory for all citizens under the age of 70. The mild penalties for failing to vote are rarely carried out.

Election campaigns resemble those in the United States, but only up to a point. All parties get equal time on national television and radio, and advertising costs are paid for with government election funds. Although campaign accusations and criticisms may be harsh and exaggerated occasionally, the personal lives of politicians are strictly off-limits during elections. Candidates stick to political issues. The mudslinging style of U.S. politics is viewed by most Costa Ricans as being undignified.

The country's long history of stability and respect for consensus discourages extreme views on either end of the political spectrum. Furthermore, flexible class distinctions and a lack of ethnic conflict lead to a kind of stability not seen in other Latin American states. Costa Rica has not had problems with overt ethnic identity politics or with Marxist political movements. Although Costa Rica's many parties span the range of political values, most tend to be centrist.

Two such centrist parties have typically won elections since the end of World War II. Don Pepe Figueres founded the National Liberation Party, or PLN. A firm commitment to maintaining Costa Rica's welfare state is a basic principle of the PLN. It tends to draw support from middle-class urban professionals and small farmers. At election time, PLN backers wave green and white flags while the colors of its main rival, the Social Christian Unity Party, or PUSC, are blue and red. The PUSC finds most of its support among larger rural landowners and more conservative urban voters. It advocates free-market principles and a reduction of government expenditures.

CONSTITUTION OF 1948

The stability of Costa Rica's democratic institutions and traditions owes much to the constitutional framework created in 1948. In that year, the Figueres government shaped the blueprint for democracy that has served the country since. Among the central features of this constitution are many guarantees familiar to U.S. citizens. Costa Ricans are guaranteed equality before the law, the right to own property, the rights of petition and assembly, freedoms of speech and of the press, and freedom of religion.

Unlike the United States, however, Costa Rica does have a state religion: Roman Catholicism. The separation of church and state is widely respected. The 1948 Constitution includes a labor code and social security provisions. Free universal education and health coverage are also guaranteed. Costa Rica's high standard of living is a result in part of the constitutional commitment to social welfare.

Perhaps the most striking aspect of the 1948 constitution is that it permanently bans the formation of a national army. The country's national hero, Don Pepe Figueres, was so committed to the idea of democracy that he pushed for this provision while temporarily ruling Costa Rica as the head of a military junta. A national domestic police force and border security forces function to maintain law and order, but a standing army has not existed since the 1940s. Costa Rican presidents reaffirm this commitment from time to time. In 1983, while much of the rest of Central America was racked by civil wars and violence, President Luis Alberto Monge proclaimed Costa Rica's permanent neutrality in all international conflicts.

FOREIGN RELATIONS

As seen before, Costa Rica shares democratic values and constitutional guarantees of civil freedoms with the United

States. On many important issues, Costa Rica has traditionally supported the United States. For example, before its ban on the formation of a standing army and its declaration of permanent neutrality, Costa Rica was the first country in the Western Hemisphere to declare war on Japan and Germany, just days after December 7, 1941. Costa Rica was also one of the only Latin America countries to immediately break off relations with Cuba in 1960, once again in a show of support for U.S. interests. Despite this long association, however, it is hardly a puppet of the United States. It is a strong advocate of arms limitation and opposes U.S. arms sales in both Latin America and around the world. Several years ago, it banned the import of all automatic weapons, many of which are made in the United States.

In terms of regional politics, Costa Rica has had serious differences with the United States over the years. The struggle to end the Central American conflicts of the 1970s and 1980s is one example. During the 1980s, Guatemala, El Salvador, and Nicaragua were all engaged in costly internal political violence. Each was fighting its own civil war against rebels, many of whom had Communist backing. National economies were stagnant.

After years of U.S. support for the repressive governments of these countries and no end to the fighting in sight, the president of Costa Rica stepped in with his own proposal for peace. President Oscar Arias, who served from 1986–1990, authored a regional peace plan in 1987 that became the Esquipulas Peace Agreement. Also known as the Central American Peace Plan, it was staunchly opposed by the United States for many reasons, not all of them easy to understand.

The Esquipulas agreement began the slow process of ending the Nicaraguan war and establishing open elections in that country. Arias also hosted negotiations between the Salvadoran government and the main rebel group in El Salvador, the FMLN, thus helping to end the war in that country. Less successfully, Arias attempted to bring warring factions together in Guatemala.

Oscar Arias, who served as Costa Rica's president from 1986 to 1990, authored the Central American Peace Plan. This was an effort to end the costly internal political violence that plagued Guatemala, El Salvador, and Nicaragua in the 1970s and 1980s.

For his efforts, Arias was awarded the 1987 Nobel Peace Prize. He used the Nobel award money to establish the Arias Foundation for Peace and Human Progress. With the long range goal of completely demilitarizing and democratizing Central America, the foundation has become an international center for the study and promotion of conflict resolution.

Although he has been out of political office for years, Oscar Arias is perhaps the most famous personality in Costa Rica today. Tour bus guides and taxi drivers proudly point out his house to visitors. International negotiators and diplomats seek his views on conflicts far from Central America. As part of the Arias legacy, President Clinton met with Central American leaders in 1997 in Costa Rica to sign the Declaration of San José. This statement of shared principles and goals made the United States a partner in Costa Rica's commitment to democracy building in Latin America.

Building on its regional experience with peacemaking, Costa Rica is now a leader in promoting international human rights issues. It lobbied for the establishment of the United Nations High Commission for Human Rights (UNHCR), and it was the first country in the world to recognize the authority of the Inter-American Human Rights Court, created in part by the UNHCR. Appropriately, the Human Rights Court is now based in San José.

Political stability, an international reputation as a center of conflict resolution, and a commitment to social welfare all come with a high price, however. Costa Rica spends a lot on providing generous services for its citizens. Currently about one in four Costa Ricans works for the government. The result is a huge financial burden. Paying off government debt currently consumes almost 30 percent of the national budget. This means less money is available for investment in other areas, such as education or transportation.

Facing the issue of international debt with the same commitment to reform that it is famous for, Costa Rica has worked to bring down barriers to free trade and open the country to world market conditions. Political leaders are finding ways to make the transition from the country's social welfare past to a future as a free trader without entirely sacrificing the heritage of socialism.

In 1998, President Miguel Rodriguez committed the country

to an austerity plan designed to bring down the national debt and attract more foreign investment. Some progress has been made. Government debt is coming down at a steady though slow rate. The political will to make these changes is still in place but the process is nevertheless painful. As the government sells off state-owned industries and deregulates banking, big changes are coming to Costa Rica. As will be seen, however, the economic benefits of shrinking the size of government are beginning to pay off as economic diversification generates new sources of wealth.

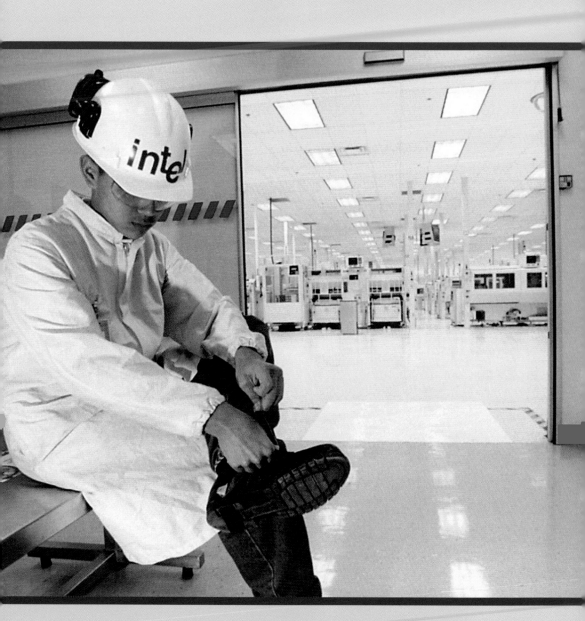

Costa Rica actively courts direct foreign investment as a means of diversifying its economy. These efforts got a boost when an American firm, Intel Corporation, invested more than $200 million in a venture to manufacture semiconductors in Costa Rica. This plant near San José employs over 2,000 people in a high-tech business that requires skilled workers. Recently, a fall in semiconductor prices has caused Intel to slow its plans for expansion.

6

Economy

C osta Rica's average annual rate of economic growth during the 1990s was the second highest in Latin America and the Caribbean. This impressive record is based on a combination of traditional economic sectors with new foreign investment and explosive growth in an industry pioneered by Costa Rica: ecotourism.

Known for over 100 years as a banana producer and for over 150 years as a world supplier of fine coffee beans, Costa Rica's agriculturally based economy is changing rapidly. As a percent of gross domestic product (GDP), the agricultural sector in 2001 represented about 9.4 percent of the national economy, while industry stood at 31.2 percent and services at 59.4 percent. By comparison, agriculture was at more than 20 percent in 1980. Growing crops for export is still important, but world prices for bananas and coffee have been depressed for much of the last twenty years. According to the World Bank, the price situation for these items will not improve much in the future. Costa Rica, however, is diversifying at a rapid pace. The country's situation midway in the Western Hemisphere makes it an ideal place for foreign investment, which, along with tourism, is shaping a new face for Costa Rica's economy.

Between 1995 and 2000, direct foreign investment (DFI) doubled to $669 million. Tax-free and duty-free export zones as well as an educated labor force attract investors from the United States and other countries. Other selling points for international business include Costa Rica's stable politics, its pleasant climate, and its proximity to North and South America. Foreign investors looking for low labor costs and short-term profits are not the norm. Companies moving to Costa Rica tend to be high-tech businesses that require skilled workers. Costa Rica's recent growth in attracting DFI got a big boost in 1998, when the U.S.-based Intel Corporation invested more than $200 million in a microprocessor finishing plant and testing facility. So far, Intel Costa Rica has created over two thousand technical and professional jobs.

The new Intel facility is located about five miles from the capital city of San José and less than two miles from the international airport. Almost all of the processors assembled and tested are shipped by air directly to North America, Europe, and Asia. The San José plant is the first of four that will eventually provide up to 5,000 jobs. It assembles and tests approximately 25 percent of all microprocessors manufactured by Intel, and this figure could go as high as 33 percent when the new facilities are completed. Intel Costa Rica won the Costa Rican-American Chamber of Commerce's 2001 Community Service Award for its corporate citizenship and commitment to worker education.

As often happens after a well-known international company invests in a country, other multinationals follow. Costa Rica quickly became Central America's most desirable location for international business. In 1999, another U.S. company, Abbott Laboratories, invested in one of Costa Rica's Free Trade Zones (FTZs). Abbott's new manufacturing facility now produces health care products for North American and Costa Rican markets. That same year, Procter and Gamble located a new global administrative service center in the country, creating nearly 1,000 new jobs. Hewlett-Packard has a small facility in the Central Valley, and Western Union and L.L. Bean now have telephone call centers in new offices outside San José.

TOURISM

Growth in ecotourism began in the 1980s and continues to generate more foreign currency than any other portion of the economy. Tourism surpassed agriculture as the largest earner of foreign exchange in 1992, and this sector has been growing steadily since, earning over $1.1 billion in 2000. As seen in the survey of Costa Rica's physical environment, the country's ecological diversity makes it a natural attraction for tourists looking for adventure or for alternatives to packaged theme park vacations.

Costa Rica's reputation as an unspoiled parkland of jungles and volcanoes did not come by accident. The government is partly responsible for the growth in tourism. Progressive political leaders have long recognized the economic potential of undeveloped mountains, unspoiled tropical beaches, and intact rain forests. In 1990, as ecotourism became a household word in North America, Costa Rica appointed its first tourism minister to the president's cabinet.

The country's far-sighted commitment to preserving natural areas has made Costa Rica one of the world's first ecotourism destinations. The commitment to national parks and low-impact "green tourism," however, is increasingly at odds with mainstream tourist development. Investors in Yucatan-style beach resort complexes are coming to Costa Rica in hopes of cashing in on the rapid growth in tourism (which is the world's largest industry). Some Costa Ricans have warned

Tourists ride through the middle layer of the rainforest canopy aboard the "Rainforest Aerial Tram" in an area 60 miles (97 kilometers) east of San José. Tourism surpassed agriculture in earning foreign currency in 1992 and is a steadily growing source of income. Political stability and physical beauty combine to create an ideal tourist destination in Costa Rica.

of the "Yucatan disease," arguing that the development of large-scale resorts will cater to a different type of tourist than the kind who comes to marvel at the country's natural beauty. In fact, that is just what is happening.

Over $1 billion in new resort development is planned in the Papagayo Gulf area alone. International resort operators such as Rosewood and Four Seasons, and golf course developers Jack Nicklaus, Arnold Palmer, and Greg Norman are all at various stages of completing Costa Rican projects. Critics point out that the new developments, and many private builders as well, violate Costa Rica's Maritime Terrestrial Zone Law, which makes the country's entire coastline public property.

Furthermore, the law prohibits construction within 50 meters of a point halfway between high and low tides. A conflict is growing between those who perceive preservation of natural beauty as a long-term economic value and those who see Costa Rica's beauty as an opportunity to cash in on travel trends.

A related economic effect of Costa Rica's natural beauty is the attraction of U.S. retirees to the country. Roughly 35,000 of them now live there year-round. Attracted by the climate, the political stability, and the favorable exchange rate, this growing number of U.S. and Canadian expatriates contributes to the growth of the service sector.

FOREIGN INVESTMENT AND FREE TRADE

In the colonial past, Spain neglected Costa Rica's develop-ment, in part because of its situation, or location relative to other parts of the Spanish New World. In the twenty-first century era of globalization, the country's relative location is now viewed as an advantage. Located midway in the hemisphere, the country is only a few hours away by air from U.S. and South American trading partners and only two days away by water. The country's leaders have long promoted free trade.

For example, Costa Rica was the leading force behind the creation of the Central American Common Market Treaty of 1960 that created duty-free trade conditions between Costa Rica, Guatemala, Honduras, El Salvador, and Nicaragua.

Costa Rica is a major proponent of the Free Trade Agree-ment of the Americas (FTAA). This U.S. plan would establish a hemispheric trading area stretching from Canada to Chile. Regardless of how the FTAA negotiations turn out in the next few years, Costa Rica also supports an extension of the North American Free Trade Agreement (NAFTA) to Central America. As well as endorsing all major U.S. trade proposals, Costa Rica acts as a regional leader in promoting free trade. It is a strong supporter of the World Trade Organization (WTO). In 1994, Costa Rica signed its own free trade agreement with Mexico. In

1998, Costa Rica joined other Central American states in establishing a Trade and Investment Council with the United States.

In a typically progressive move, the government established Free Trade Zones (FTZs) in 1981. The first two FTZs were industrial parks in Puntarenas and Puerto Limón that offered foreign companies reduced taxes, land rents, and access to port facilities. Today, eight FTZs operate in the country. Under free trade rules of the WTO, these will have to be phased out over the next few years since they give the country an unfair advantage in attracting foreign investment. Currently, 219 foreign companies, most of them U.S.-based, employ over 31,000 Costa Rican workers. In the 1990s, electronics assembly plants led the way in FTZ investment. About 69 percent of FTZ firms make electronics for export. Textile plants are in second place at about 9 percent of the total.

The United States is Costa Rica's most important trading and investment partner. In terms of exports and imports combined, the United States enjoys about 54 percent of Costa Rica's total trade. The European Union (EU) has 21.3 percent and other Central American countries 8.6 percent. In 2001, Costa Rica imported about $3.4 billion in U.S. goods and services, more than 53 percent of its total imports. In terms of investment, more than 64 percent of FDI from 1985 to 2000 came from U.S. companies. At least half of the roughly 1.2 million tourists who visit each year are United States citizens. The only significant import sector that is not U.S.-based is petroleum. The country has a dozen hydroelectric plants, but Costa Rica still must import oil to meet growing energy demands.

These connections to the United States are growing stronger as the country diversifies. For example, a consortium led by the U.S. firm Bechtel took over management of Costa Rica's principal airport in May 2001. Under a twenty-year contract, the consortium will continue to modernize and upgrade air services linking Costa Rica to North American tourists and investors.

Because of government support for education, the labor

force is well trained. Success at attracting foreign investors has, however, created a shortage of skilled English-speaking workers. Although Costa Rica has more English speakers than any other Central American country, the recent moves by Intel, Procter and Gamble, and the new Western Union call center have depleted the supply of fluent business and technical English speakers.

Other indications of North American influence may be found on the cultural landscape. U.S.-style franchises are becoming common, as are shopping centers and malls. McDonald's was the first U.S. franchise to open in 1970. Now such familiar brands as Pizza Hut, Blockbuster Video, and Outback Steakhouse are located in San José and several of the country's bigger cities. More than 80 percent of these franchises are foreign owned, almost all by U.S. investors.

As well as attracting investment from the United States, Costa Rica also buys many products from the United States. For example, the number one industrial import from the United States is paper and paperboard products that are used primarily in agricultural exports. In some import sectors, the United States dominates; over 90 percent of Costa Rica's computers and computer equipment come from the United States. Almost all telecommunications equipment is made in the United States.

The United States also exports agricultural products to Costa Rica. Soybeans and corn used for feed in the expanding poultry and dairy industries top the list, but the United States also sells increasing amounts of wheat and rice. Unless the United States acts to match Costa Rica's commitment to free trade, a slight decline in some U.S. agricultural imports may be seen in the near future. Costa Rica imports apples, grapes, pears, and peaches from both the United States and Chile. Chile exports these items typically in the Northern Hemisphere's winter and early spring—the harvest season in the Southern Hemisphere. As Chile enters its winter season, U.S. harvests begin and so Costa Rica enjoys a year-round supply of fresh fruit. However, Costa Rica is negotiating a free trade agreement with Chile that would reduce U.S. competitiveness.

Another important import sector is agricultural chemicals. Costa Rica's government has long supported export agriculture with banking credits and other incentives. Because of the low productivity of tropical soils, demand for fertilizers, fungicides, herbicides, and pesticides is high. Costa Rica produces no agro-chemicals or fertilizers and depends entirely on imports. The U.S. supplies about one-third of these vital tools in the battle against tropical crop diseases, fungus, and nematodes (worms).

AGRICULTURE

In the traditional agricultural sector, bananas and coffee dominate Costa Rica's exports, but cattle ranching is growing steadily. In terms of land use, nearly 70 percent of agricultural land is devoted to cattle. Guanacaste in the northwest is the center of the cattle industry, as it has been since the seventeenth century. Approximately 75 percent of Costa Rica's 2.2 million cattle are there. For many years, Guanacaste ranchers raised Zebus, the distinctive ox-like Asian breed that is adapted to tropical climates.

After World War II, North American breeds such as Charolais and Herefords became popular. The country is now the leading beef exporter in Central America, selling more and more beef to North America. This expansion comes at a high price, however. Once cleared of trees for grazing, tropical soils quickly become infertile. Soil erosion and flooding are common problems where cattle ranching is practiced in tropical climates.

Costa Rica's first significant export crop was coffee, and the country is still famous for producing high-quality beans. Most of the country's small and medium-sized coffee fincas are located in the Central Valley, which is ideal for production. Higher-quality beans are grown near the upper limits of the coffee plant's altitudinal tolerance, between roughly 2,500 and 5,000 feet (762 to 1,524 meters) above sea level. Here, the

Workers measure freshly harvested coffee on a finca near Naranjo, which is 37 miles (60 kilometers) west of San José. In 2001, Costa Rica hosted a conference for twenty-nine of the world's coffee-producing nations during International Coffee Week.

average annual temperature range is narrow and rainfall is seasonal. The short dry season, combined with the relatively cool nights and warm days of the tierra templada, produce some of the world's best Arabica coffee.

As with other agricultural commodities, international market prices for coffee fluctuate from year to year, depending on weather conditions and competition from other producers. World production doubled between 1970 and 2000, but per capita coffee consumption declined slightly over the same period. In an attempt to bring stability to the market, coffee producers formed a cartel in the 1980s. Cartels are agreements between producers that regularize production and set export levels and prices. Unlike members of another famous cartel, the

Organization of Petroleum Exporting Countries (OPEC), the members of the coffee cartel didn't cooperate on exports.

After several years of exceptionally good harvests, Brazil sabotaged the International Coffee Agreement in 1989 by exceeding its national export quotas. The world coffee market was flooded with inexpensive Brazilian coffee and prices fell sharply. The result was that Costa Rica and other small Central American producers lost much of their share of the international market.

Coffee and bananas are still the mainstays of the agricultural sector. Sugar cane and cacao (from which chocolate is derived) are also important crops in some parts of the tierra caliente. Although the agricultural sector's share of GDP falls slightly each year, this decline should be seen in context of the growth of tourism and industry. Most years, Costa Rica is still the second- or third-biggest banana exporter in the world, supplying much of the North American market. Just as coffee farmers face increased competition from new coffee-producing countries in Africa and Asia, the banana sector also faces increased competition. The so-called banana war of the 1990s highlights the intersection of agricultural competition and the complex political issues of free trade.

The United States and the European Union are the largest banana importers in the world. Much of the EU's banana imports come from former English and French colonies that are able to import their product into European markets duty-free under a special trade agreement. These producers, primarily African and Caribbean countries, thus have an unfair advantage over so-called "dollar bananas" (those grown in Central and South America by U.S. companies). In 1997, some of these producers along with the United States filed a complaint with the World Trade Organization. The WTO ruled that the EU banana import system was unfair. The EU has agreed in principle to phase out the price structure favoring former colonies, but so far little actual change has occurred, and the dispute simmers on.

Unlike coffee production, which mostly takes place on small family-owned fincas, bananas are grown on large monoculture (raising only one cash crop) plantations. Dole, Chiquita, and other international companies own most of these land-intensive operations. Bananas are subject to devastation by tropical storms, hurricanes, and tropical fungal diseases. Small growers are disadvantaged by the fact that they cannot absorb major losses as easily as big agribusiness.

Before effective agro-chemicals were developed, diseases such as black and yellow Sigatoka, or leaf streak, and Panama disease routinely wiped out banana crops in Central America. These fungal diseases reduce a plant's ability to capture the sun's energy, reducing the production of bananas by 50 percent or more. At one point, Panama disease was so widespread in Costa Rica that the United Fruit Company moved its operations to Honduras and Guatemala, though it still bought bananas from independent Costa Rican producers. In 1938, Sigatoka disease struck Costa Rica and the UFC temporarily stopped purchases.

Black Sigatoka can be controlled with fungicides, but this is an expensive option. The annual cost of fungicide applications is about $1,000 per 2.4 acres (1 hectare). Roughly 15–20 percent of the retail price of bananas in North America and Europe pays for agro-chemicals. Independent small growers usually cannot afford the high cost. They rely on traditional methods: removing diseased leaves by hand and flooding the land to clear the soil of the disease. In Honduras, geneticists are developing new experimental banana hybrids that will be resistant to Sigatoka. The banana breeding program offers hope that banana growers will one day reduce their dependence on agro-chemicals.

The next chapter surveys the regional changes that are underway as economic diversification and tourist development bring new wealth and opportunity to Costa Rica.

Carlos Chaverri Alpizar, of Sarchi, Costa Rica, is a third-generation resident who is famous all over the world for his painted *carreras*, or oxcarts. From the seventeenth to the twentieth century, the carrera transported coffee and other crops to market, but now that they are no longer used they have become an art form and a staple of the tourist trade.

7

Regional Contrasts

The chapter on natural landscapes examined the physical regions of Costa Rica and noted the sharp differences in the country's altitudinal zones. The political units will now be analyzed to obtain a sense of the economic and social differences. Although this is a country with a keen sense of cultural unity and a high degree of cultural homogenization, some regional variations do exist.

Costa Rica is comprised of seven provinces that vary in physical size and population. When thinking about the provincial divisions, keep in mind that modern political boundaries usually do not take into account natural features. Political boundaries are generally the most precise type of line drawn on a map, but they frequently cut across physical features such as mountain ranges or bodies of water. Several examples can be seen by looking at regional contrasts.

ALAJUELA

With a population of about 594,000, the province of Alajuela is the second most populous in the country. In physical extent, it is also the third largest, comprising 3,766 square miles (9,754 square kilometers). Most of the province lies on the northern side of the central volcanic mountain range. Numerous streams and rivers with mountain headwaters flow northward into the San Juan River or into Lake Nicaragua just over the border. The vast lowlands territory north of the mountains extends to the Nicaraguan border and until recently was covered in dense rain forest. The lack of roads throughout this area set it apart from the densely populated Central Mountains in the southern part of the province. Recent road construction and the expansion of cattle ranching into the lowlands has resulted in the clearing of significant portions of this heavily forested area.

Alajuela also incorporates portions of the Guanacaste Mountains in the far northwest, but it is the Central Mountain range and the western part of the Central Valley that the population is concentrated. Descendents of some of the country's earliest settlers who migrated out of the colonial core in the eastern part of the Central Valley live in small towns and the capital city of Alajuela (population 160,000). Finding the same kind of productive volcanic soils as in the eastern valley, these settlers began farming the tierra templada as they had in the east. Today, much of Costa Rica's corn, beans, and vegetable are grown here, as well as coffee.

Along with agriculture, tourism underpins the provincial economy. Six national parks and wildlife refuges, including the famous Arenal National Park, are located here. Tourists are also drawn by the highland culture of Costa Rica. In this end of the Central Valley, far from the urban highlands of San José, one may get a sense of the country's recent history. Beautiful nineteenth-century architecture can be found in the provincial capital as well as in the small towns. Villages such as Sarchí attract tourists looking for rural highland crafts.

About one hundred years ago, a coffee mill worker in the village of Sarchí painted the sides and wooden wheels of a traditional oxcart, or *carreta*, with colorful designs. From the seventeenth to the twentieth century, the carreta was the only means of transporting coffee and other crops to market. The painted carreta was adopted throughout the country, becoming a national symbol of small town life and traditions. The days of the oxcarts are long gone, of course, but today the production of miniature hand-painted oxcarts for the tourist trade is an important local industry.

CARTAGO

The small, landlocked province of Cartago lies almost entirely on the Atlantic side of the continental divide, so most of the region is wet year-round. The city of Cartago, however, sits in the rain shadow of the towering, 11,260 feet (3,432 meters) Irazú Volcano, and receives far less rainfall. At an elevation of 4,721 feet (1,439 meters), the city's weather is pleasantly mild year-round. One of the country's most popular natural attractions is Irazú Volcano National Park, less than an hour's drive from the city limits. Irazú's regular, low-key eruptions light up the night sky and create a spectacular display of pyrotechnics for tourists. Although safe from Irazú's fire, the city has been struck five times by earthquakes, the most recent and most destructive being the 1910 quake.

The city of Cartago is the site of the earliest permanent Spanish settlement in the country. Formerly the colonial capital of Costa Rica, Cartago was chosen by Coronado for its rich agricultural potential and mild climate (the capital of the newly independent Costa Rica was moved to San José in 1823.)

Along with the rest of the Central Valley, Cartago may be considered the cultural core of Costa Rica. For almost three hundred years after the establishment of the colony, practically all of the wealth and people of Costa Rica were located in the

Valley. The highest population densities are still found there today. This was the source area for the settlement pattern that extended throughout the Central Valley and beyond throughout the nineteenth and early twentieth centuries. The colonial highland culture that spread throughout the valley has its roots here. Today, the province ranks third in population, with 350, 000 people.

GUANACASTE

Guanacaste is the second-largest province in area, comprising slightly more than 3,860 square miles (10,000 square kilometers). Despite its size, it has the second-smallest population in Costa Rica. Although it has grown steadily since the end of World War II, only about 250,000 people live there today. The provincial capital, Liberia, has fewer than 38,000 people.

Most of Guanacaste is tropical dry forest, like much of the Pacific coast from southern Mexico to the Panamanian border. It is by far the driest region in the country. Except for the mountains in the northeast, rainfall is seasonal. During the late fall and winter months, northeast trade winds out of the Caribbean are forced up over the continental divide, producing orographic precipitation (rain from clouds forced up the sides of mountains). After the moisture has been wrung from them, these now-dry winds sweep across Guanacaste's Pacific slope and stop any wet Pacific air masses from making landfall.

As seen in the chapter on Costa Rica's history, Guanacaste has always been somewhat different from the other provinces in terms of ethnicity. At the time of European exploration, it had the highest Indian population of any region in the country, and intermarriage between Spanish and natives was common. Today, about half the population is mestizo, the highest rate of any province. Culturally, the region resembles neighboring Nicaragua as much as it does Costa Rica. In fact, Guanacaste was originally part of Nicaragua. It was annexed by Costa Rica shortly after Central American independence from Spain on July 25, 1825. The day is now a national holiday.

In Guanacaste, the second largest province in Costa Rica, tourism and ranching are important to the economy. Cattle ranching has been part of the culture since the 1600s.

Recently an influx of Americans who come to build retirement homes and beach houses has begun changing the character of the coastal areas. The relatively unspoiled beaches at Playa del Coco, Playa Potrero, and Tamarindo Beach are also under pressure from resort developers. Hotels, golf courses, and large-scale resort complexes are springing up. With a new international airport in Liberia, Guanacaste is only a couple of hours away from the United States, and these new developments will likely spawn more of the same in the near future. The new resorts do not necessarily cater to the "green tourists" of the 1990s who came looking for outdoor adventure or exotic bird watching. The new travel development is designed to appeal to mass tourist travelers, people who spend their vacation time within the confines of planned packaged trips.

Sugar cane, rice, and cotton are important local crops, but tourism and ranching are the biggest economic activities. Long an exporter of beef, Guanacaste's cattle culture stretches back to the early 1600s. A cowboy museum in Liberia showcases the province's colorful ranching history. During the early nineteenth century, for instance, it was the starting point for several cattle drives to the markets in Guatemala, over 350 miles away! The expanding cattle industry means a stable export economy for the province, but the environmental effects are not sustainable. Guanacaste may be reaching the ecological limits of ranching.

HEREDIA

The smallest province in Costa Rica is Heredia. Occupying a portion of the Central Valley and the Central Mountain range, the province also includes Caribbean slope jungles that extend north of the mountains to the border with Nicaragua. Within this small area, about 1,025 square miles (2,655 square kilometers), some of the most varied topography and vegetation anywhere in the country is found. Conditions range from the steaming rain forest of the San Juan River lowlands, to the mild Central Valley, and to the cool mountains in the south.

Most of the province's 240,000 people are scattered in small towns in the tierra templada, like the populations of the other highland provinces. Like other parts of the Central Valley and highlands, the city of Heredia (population, 70,000) is part of the country's culture hearth. The first town to be established outside of the Cartago area was not far from the present-day site of the city of Heredia. Named after an early settler, the city is also the location of one of the country's oldest surviving church structures, dating back to 1797, and to other examples of colonial architecture.

Heredia is also the hearth of Costa Rica's coffee production. When coffee was introduced as a cash crop, the seasonal dryness, volcanic soils, and mild temperatures attracted some of the first coffee growers to this part of the valley. Descendents of some of these first coffee families continue to work coffee fincas on and near the slopes of Barva Volcano.

Puerto Limón is the capital of the province of Limón, which extends the length of the Atlantic, or Caribbean, coast of Costa Rica. At one time bananas were the leading export crop, but today most banana exports come from the Pacific lowlands.

LIMÓN

The province of Limón extends the length of Costa Rica's Atlantic, or Caribbean, coast, from the mouth of the San Juan River on the Nicaraguan border, to the Sixaola River on the border with Panama. The least populated of the seven provinces, Limón's 220,000 people are scattered in small settlements, mainly close to the coast. The largest city, Puerto Limón, has a population of about 70,000. Many of the biggest parks and reserves are located in this sparsely inhabited region. Most of Limón is very hot year-round with extensive tracts of old banana and cacao plantations, but the province also includes the country's highest peak, Mt. Chirrip. It is the only province to sit entirely on the Caribbean side of the continental divide.

Although perfect for growing bananas, Limón's dominant climate, the tierra caliente, has never attracted people in great numbers. The constant high heat and humidity of most of the region made it a poor place for settlement, and transportation routes between the densely settled Central Valley and the lush rain forest along the coast were nonexistent. A few cacao farms were established in the eighteenth century. After their decline, some tobacco was grown, but the region did not see much development until the government undertook plans to link the fertile coffee sections beyond the continental divide with the Caribbean coast.

This link was finally completed in 1891 when Minor Keith's Atlantic rail line was completed. During the construction of the railroad, Keith also established the first banana plantations in the country, and this crop quickly became Limón's leading agricultural industry. As seen in the survey of ethnicity, Limón today is home to the descendents of Jamaicans who came to work on the railroad and on the banana plantations.

The provincial capital of Puerto Limón was founded in 1867. According to local historians, a lemon tree was growing on the spot where the town was laid out, hence the name Limón. The Atlantic railroad made Puerto Limón the world's premier banana port for much of the early twentieth century, and the region has grown slowly since then. Bananas are still grown on large plantations, although much of the country's banana exports now come from the Pacific lowlands. Some of the old banana lands have been converted to cacao production.

PUNTARENAS

Puntarenas is the largest province in Costa Rica, encompassing about 4,350 square miles (11,267 square kilometers). Somewhat like Limón on the Caribbean side of the central cordillera, Puntarenas was isolated from the settlements of the Central Valley until the twentieth century. The province's shape on the map, winding up from the Panamanian border in the south to curl around most of the Gulf of Nicoya, reflects this historical isolation. This coastal zone developed its own regional variation of the national culture throughout the eighteenth and nineteenth centuries when communication and contact with the interior was sporadic.

The province lies entirely on the Pacific side of the continental divide, but unlike Guanacaste to the north, it is not as affected by seasonal dryness. In fact, most of the southern portion has no true dry season. For this reason, it attracted the Atlantic banana growers who came in the 1930s and 1940s in a vain attempt to escape the Sigatoka disease that was ravaging the Caribbean plantations. The new plantations along the southern coast created thousands of jobs in the 1940s, and the population of the province began to grow dramatically. The ports of Golfito and Quepos were built to expedite banana exports. When Sigatoka made its way to the Pacific in the mid-1950s, some of the banana plantations were converted to growing African oil palm, which is used to produce cooking and cosmetic oils. Oil palm farming is now a slowly growing but stable aspect of Puntarenas agriculture.

The older port town of Puntarenas was developed after coffee became a significant export crop in the 1840s. Long transported to the coast on oxcart trails, coffee exports were boosted when a railroad to San José was completed in 1910. In the 1980s a new port was built for the larger ships that are now the norm in international sea trade.

As in most other provinces, tourism is the biggest money-maker in Puntarenas. Some of Costa Rica's most popular beach resorts are along the southwestern coast. The province is also home to more parks and reserves than any other part of the country. An important aspect of Caribbean Island tourism, sea cruise tours, has recently become part of Costa Rica's tourist economy. Port Caldera, on the Gulf of Nicoya, now attracts cruise liners. These large ships dock for short periods of time, giving passengers an opportunity to visit the coast.

SAN JOSÉ

San José is the most densely populated province, and in total numbers, the biggest. Its 1.2 million residents live in and around the Central Valley with the most significant population clustered around the national capital of San José. Most of the people live in a band of elevation between 2,300 and 4,300 (700 and 1,310 meters) above sea level. This is classic tierra templada, with year-round mild temperatures and adequate rainfall for coffee and vegetable production.

Along with other cities of the Central Valley, the San José metropolitan area is part of the cultural hearth of old Costa Rica, but the province also includes sparsely populated areas. Examples of each kind of altitudinal zone found in Costa Rica are located here. Although most of San José's territory lies on the high Pacific slopes of the Central and Talamanca Mountains, the province also extends close to the Pacific coast in several places.

As well as being the capital of the country, the city of San José is the core of Costa Rica's new export economy. Most of the recent foreign investment is in plants and facilities located within a few miles of the city. Almost all of the new jobs in microprocessor and electronics manufacturing are here. Transnational companies are attracted by the area's developed infrastructure, such as the modern international airport, the mild climate, and the province's natural beauty.

The San José metropolitan area is home to 1.2 million residents and is the most densely populated part of the country.

San José was made the national capital after a brief civil war in 1823. The war, a mild one by regional standards, broke out after independence from Spain. During this time, Costa Rica was a country of small highland towns. Economic and political competition was sometimes intense. Most citizens of the towns of San José and Alajuela wanted independence; the citizens of Cartago and Heredia favored confederation with Mexico. Supporters of independence won, and the capital was moved from Cartago to San José.

Costa Rican schoolgirls plant saplings as part of an Earth Day celebration in San José. Planting new trees is a step toward the goal of preserving and regenerating the tropical forests for future generations.

Costa Rica
Looks Ahead

The discussion of Costa Rica began with a look at the combination of luck and vision that makes the country unique. To get a sense of where the people of Costa Rica are going in the future, focus now shifts to an institution built on the good fortune of the past and a visionary commitment to the future: Costa Rica's Earth University.

Dedicated to the study of "sustainable agricultural management of the humid tropics," Earth University began in 1984 with an initiative by leaders in agriculture and education. The Costa Rican government passed a bill creating the institution, and, with funding from the U.S. Agency for International Development, construction of the campus began in Guacimo in 1989. The school opened its doors on March 26, 1990, with sixty students. Now, one hundred new students are admitted to the program each year, most of them from Latin America and Spain. As the school's research in tropical agriculture and forestry become better known, more students are coming from other tropical regions of the world. Recently, students from Uganda have been attracted by the school's tropical expertise. Since 1994, Earth University has graduated 715 agricultural management and natural resource professionals.

According to the university's website, the school's educational model is based on "four pillars: social commitment, environmental awareness, an entrepreneurial mentality, and the development of human values." An example of a university project that brings together these values is its 750-acre (304 hectares) banana plantation. Here, students have the opportunity to research sustainable banana agriculture. One of their programs is the production of paper from discarded banana stems (traditionally, a bulky and troublesome waste by-product of monoculture banana plantations). The success of this program earned Earth's banana farm the ECO-OK seal of approval from the Rainforest Alliance.

On June 11th, 2002, the faculty and students held the annual Planting Trees Day. The event attracted nearly 600 people who planted 12,000 trees on land owned by the university. Since the event began, in 1995, the school's students have reforested 145 acres (60 hectares) on the Planting Trees Days, and an additional 1,300 acres (526 hectares) in other reforestation projects. Planting Trees Day focuses attention on the institution's goal of preserving and regenerating tropical forests.

Forest health and agricultural sustainability are long-term goals requiring a visionary commitment to patience, hard work, and the general welfare of people and ecosystems. In this regard, Earth University reflects Costa Rica's national traits and progressive values.

Working for sustainability is a serious undertaking in an uncertain world of rapid economic change and political turmoil. Another example of Costa Rica's national tendency to make long-range commitments can be found in the coffee industry. Lucky in the past to have a climate and soils ideal for coffee, the country faces some problems with maintaining its coffee export revenues. According to the World Bank, world coffee prices will probably recover from the decline of the past five years by the year 2004, but the historically high prices of the 1970s will never return.

Competition in the industry from new producing states such as Vietnam and a number of African countries means that the market will continue to be volatile. North America and European coffee consumption rates are stagnant, and analysts claim consumption will never return to its previous high rates of the 1970s and 1980s. What Costa Rica has done in the face of these realities is to specialize in high-quality coffee production. Now a world leader in organically grown beans, Costa Rica is refining its economic niche in the coffee trade. The country may not increase its share of the world market, but it will sustain its tradition of coffee farming while adjusting to new market conditions.

In the realm of foreign investment, Costa Rica faces uncertainties too. In 2001, a fall in semiconductor prices slowed Intel's expansion of its Costa Rican investments. New facilities slated for construction have been delayed until prices rise again. Almost 40 percent of Costa Rica's exports are now semiconductors, so the world slowdown seriously affected the national economy as well as delaying the plans of other foreign investors.

The other major sector of the economy, the tourism industry, slumped dramatically after September 11, 2001. Already the number of travelers is on the rise again, but the severe drop in tourist dollars, like the slowdown in semiconductors, points out vulnerabilities in the economy.

The twenty-first century looks good, nevertheless. Already self-sufficient in energy needs (except for gasoline), Costa Rica exports hydroelectric power to Nicaragua. When a modern distribution grid system is developed for the region, it could become a major exporter of electricity to other countries in Central America.

No one knows what the future may hold, but if Costa Rica maintains its sense of identity and follows its democratic instincts, it will serve as a model for other rapidly developing countries. Its reputation as a leader in natural lands preservation and in conflict resolution already highlights the two global issues of our new century—securing peace and ensuring environmental health.

Facts at a Glance

Land and People

Official Name	Republic of Costa Rica
Location	Central America, that portion of Middle America located between Mexico and South America; bordered by the Pacific Ocean and the Caribbean Sea
Area	19,652 square miles (50, 899 square kilometers), about the size of West Virginia
Climate	Wet tropical, wet-and-dry tropical, and tropical highland
Capital	San José
Other Cities	Alajuela, Puntarenas, Puerto Limón, Cartago
Population	3.95 million (2002, est.)
Major Rivers	San Juan (along Nicaraguan border), San Carlos, Sarapiqui
Mountains	Cordillera Central (continental divide), Talamanca Mountains
Official Language	Spanish
Religion	Roman Catholic
Literacy Rate	94% (1998 est.)
Average Life Expectancy	74 years

Economy

Natural Resources	Hydropower
Agricultural Products	Coffee, bananas, rice, timber, sugar, cattle
Industries	Microprocessors, food processing, textiles and clothing, construction materials, plastic products
Major Imports	Machinery, vehicles, consumer goods, chemicals, petroleum products
Major Exports	Coffee, bananas, beef, textiles, fruits, sugar, flowers
Major Trading Partners	United States, European Union, other Central American countries, Japan
Currency	Colones

Government

Form of Government	Democratic republic
Government Bodies	Unicameral legislative assembly
Formal Head of State	President
Voting Rights	18 and older, compulsory

1502	Christopher Columbus lands on Costa Rica's Caribbean coast on his fourth voyage to the New World.
1522	The Davila expedition names the region Costa Rica, "the Rich Coast."
1560	Spain places the Central American isthmus under the jurisdiction of the colonial administrative center in Guatemala.
1563	Juan Vásquez de Coronado appointed Costa Rica's first governor. He establishes the city of Cartago as the colonial capital.
1706	Heredia is founded.
1709	Uprising of indigenous people in the Talamanca region.
1723	Irazú Volcano erupts, threatening the city of Cartago.
1736	San José is founded.
1782	Alajuela is founded.
1821	Spain's Central American colonies declare their independence with the Act of September 15, 1821. The Central American Republic, composed of Mexico, Guatemala, El Salvador, Honduras, and Costa Rica is formed.
1824	Guanacaste, formerly a part of Nicaragua, becomes Costa Rica's seventh province.
1825	Costa Rica's first coffee shipment leaves the country.
1839	The Central American Republic formally dissolves.
1843	Costa Rica's first university, University of Santo Tomás, is founded in San José.
1846	Oxcart road from the Central Valley coffee farms to Puntarenas is completed. Coffee exports increase.
1870	Construction begins on railroad from Central Valley to the Caribbean coast. Shipping coffee from the Atlantic side of the country cuts coffee prices in half.
1878	Costa Rica becomes the first Central American republic to grow and export bananas.
1882	Death penalty abolished.
1891	The Atlantic rail line completed.
1910	An earthquake destroys Cartago.

1940 Costa Rica's largest public university, University of Costa Rica, is founded.

1948 Protesting a fraudulent presidential election, José (Don Pepe) Figueres overthrows the government and heads a military junta for 18 months, then turns the government over to the elected president. Reforms are enacted such as the constitutional ban on a standing army.

1963 Irazú Volcano erupts, shrouding the Central Valley with ash and destroying crops.

1968 Arenal Volcano erupts, killing 78 people.

1970 The Department of National Parks is created.

1983 President Luis Alberto Monge proclaims permanent neutrality.

1987 Costa Rican President Oscar Arias wins the Nobel Peace Prize for his Central American Peace Plan.

1997 Intel begins making computer microprocessors in Costa Rica. Other foreign investors are attracted by the climate, stability, and location of the country.

2000 Tourism brings over $1.1 billion into the economy.

Further Reading

Mavis Hiltunen Biesanz, Richard Biesanz, Karen Zubris Biesanz, 1998. *The Ticos: Culture and Social Change in Costa Rica*. Lynne Rienner Publishers.

Sterling Evans, 1999. *The Green Republic: A Conservation History of Costa Rica*. University of Texas Press.

Joseph Franke, 1999. *Costa Rica's National Parks and Preserves: A Visitor's Guide* (2nd Edition). Mountaineers Books.

Chalene Helmuth, 2000. *Culture and Customs of Costa Rica (Culture and Customs of Latin America and the Caribbean)*. Greenwood Publishing Group.

Carrol L. Henderson, Steve Adams (Illustrator), Alexander F. Skutch, 2002. *Field Guide to the Wildlife of Costa Rica*. University of Texas Press.

Daniel H. Janzen (Editor), 1983. *Costa Rican Natural History*. University of Chicago Press.

Twan Leenders, 2001. *A Guide to Amphibians and Reptiles of Costa Rica*. Distribuidores Zona Tropical, S.A.

Nalini M. Nadkarni and Nathaniel T. Wheelwright (Editors), 2000. *Monteverde: Ecology and Conservation of a Tropical Cloud Forest*. Getty Center for Education in the Arts.

Harry S. Pariser, 2000. *Explore Costa Rica*. Manatee Press.

Rob Rachowiecki and John Thompson, 2000. *Lonely Planet Costa Rica* (4th Edition) Lonely Planet.

Deborah Sick, 1999. *Farmers of the Golden Bean: Costa Rican Households and the Global Coffee Economy*. Northern Illinois University Press.

F. Gary Stiles, Alexander F. Skutch (Contributor), Dana Gardner (Illustrator), 1990. *A Guide to the Birds of Costa Rica*. Cornell University Press.

Bruce M. Wilson, 1998. *Costa Rica: Politics, Economics, and Democracy*. Lynne Rienner Publishers.

Bibliography

PRINT REFERENCES

Global Economic Prospects and the Developing Countries. Washington, D.C.: The World Bank, 2002.

Merriam-Webster's Geographical Dictionary (third edition) 1998. Springfield: Merriam-Webster, Incorporated.

INTERNET REFERENCES

CIA World Factbook 2000. Country Listing for Costa Rica
  [http://www.odci.gov/cia/publications/factbook/index.html]

Earth University.
  [http://www.earth.ac.cr/]

U.S. Department of State, Bureau of Western Hemisphere Affairs. Background Note: Costa Rica.
  [http://www.state.gov/r/pa/ei/bgn/2019.htm]

U.S. Commercial Service. Costa Rica Country Commercial Guide FY2002.
  [http://www.usatrade.gov/website/ccg.nsf/CCGurl/CCG-COSTA _RICA2002-CH—00685069]

World Bank. Costa Rica Data Profile.
  [http://devdata.worldbank.org/external/dgprofile.asp?rmdk=82630&w=0& L=E]

Index

Index

Picture Credits

page:

ROGER DENDINGER was born in New Orleans. He is an associate professor of geography at the South Dakota School of Mines and Technology.

CHARLES F. ("FRITZ") GRITZNER is Distinguished Professor of Geography at South Dakota University in Brookings. He is now in his fifth decade of college teaching and research. During his career, he has taught more than 60 different courses, spanning the fields of physical, cultural, and regional geography. In addition to his teaching, he enjoys writing, working with teachers, and sharing his love for geography with students. As consulting editor for the MODERN WORLD NATIONS series, he has a wonderful opportunity to combine each of these "hobbies." Fritz has served as both president and executive director of the National Council for Geographic Education and has received the Council's highest honor, the George J. Miller Award for Distinguished Service.